WALK
THE
WALK

PETE GILBERT

WALK THE WALK

RADICAL HOLINESS THROUGH DISCIPLESHIP

CONTENTS

Dedication

This book is dedicated to my family – my wife Nikki and my daughter Freddi and son Joshua. Also to my close friends – they know who they are! Together these people have discipled me and still do.

My thanks go also to the many contributors to the DNA Discipleship programme for some of the material here, particularly to Chris Wincott, Rich and Ness Wilson, John Barr, Andy Horne and Pete Birch. The good stuff is theirs, the errors are mine!

INTRODUCTION

There's a certain inevitability about pregnancy – what's inside, must come out! You can *talk* about having a baby, about parenting, budgeting, names and nurseries for nine months, but eventually, talking the talk is not enough! Nothing, I've found, prepares you for the reality other than *doing* it! You have to walk the walk!

Forgive my using a personal analogy of pregnancy but you see I have written this book for you and I want you to hear my heart. I want to relate to you some of my experiences, so that you can see and feel that it's real and it works; that you can avoid some of the mistakes that I have made over the years. So we may as well start this introduction with personal illustration, as I mean to continue. Not that I've ever been pregnant, you understand! But my wife has.

It was a Friday morning in mid-June. The date had been marked in my diary and etched on my memory for nine months. Of course, everyone had said the baby (our second) would come early, and what with all the stress of moving house to plant a church into Portsmouth, the baby was surely bound to arrive early. We had only moved house less than three weeks before. So I had created space in my diary to help with the unpacking and to be near my wife Nikki – all in anticipation of an early arrival.

What's inside must come out! But babies come when they are good and ready and not before! And Joshua James (unlike his sister Frederica Clare, who arrived three weeks late!) decided to arrive on the actual due date. Of course, I had gone off to a meeting that eventful Friday morning, hadn't I? I mean, they never actually arrive on the due date, do they? So when Nikki phoned at 9.50 am and said, 'You'd better come now, contractions are strong and every two minutes', I was 54 miles away and panicking! I shouldn't tell you how long it took me to get home (40 minutes!). But to cut a long story short Joshua James was born at 4.48 pm, weighing in at 9 lbs 11 oz and I *was* there!

And the point is? The point is that through Josh's birth I was to learn a lot about safe and clean delivery in a protected environment. The fact is that the first ten minutes of Josh's life were the worst ten minutes of mine. I am not sure how to put this politely; he'd actually filled his nappy whilst still in his mother's womb, except of course he wasn't wearing a nappy! Consequently he had to be suctioned once delivered. The problem was that they couldn't get a suction tube down him and so they couldn't get him breathing. And to compound matters, as he went bluer and bluer in front of my eyes, the hospital paediatrician, due to a hospital error, didn't arrive for ten minutes!

What's all that to you? Well, my hope is that you picked up this book because of the title and its strap line. I am utterly convinced that there is a radical new generation of people carrying the divine spark of new life. You have been, to use Jesus' words, 'born again'. You are, to use Paul's words, 'not ashamed of the gospel'. But the critical thing for you now is to turn words into action, talk into walk, to get what God has put on the inside of you outside, so that you can, not only believe it, not only experience it, but actually live it out. Not only live it out, but actually give it away.

Forgive my bluntness, but I have written this book in order to minimise the number of Christian stillbirths and post-natal mortalities. To ensure that if you need any muck suctioned out of your life, that that can happen as quickly, yet as thoroughly as possible. Why? So that you might become a radically holy disciple who pleases Jesus Christ. Discipleship never happens in a vacuum, always in a context. The context is meant to be a safe one, where problems can be diagnosed and overcome. The context of personal radical discipleship is interpersonal radical relationships. Your safe context for nurture and growth is, like my son Joshua's, the family – the Church of Jesus Christ.

The chances are that if you are reading this book you may well represent a generation (call them Generation XY or Z, call them what you will), where largely the absolutes have been denied. Where right and wrong has become relative. Where behavioural parameters are being abandoned in favour of 'experience is all', and where the increasing poverty and irrelevance of institutions and even history itself have produced a sense of disconnection and rootlessness. Your generation is tired of 'talk only' Christianity.

Yet you are also part of a generation, perhaps more than any that have gone before, who understand and reach towards the importance of relationships. Who are not conned by the destitution of the solutions offered by technology, materialism or mere organised religion. A generation who strive towards relevant shared experiential spirituality. And now you have discovered as a Christian that there still is a meta-narrative. There is a BIG picture. God IS. And God is LOVE. And God has loved YOU. And called you to radical holiness. You want desperately to walk the walk.

So, I have written this book in an attempt to do two things. Firstly, to establish exactly what God has done for you on the inside. What is the extent and scope of this wonderful gospel of Jesus Christ, the Gospel of Freedom? To discover what in your wildest dreams you always hoped for and probably tasted when you first met with Jesus – that following Jesus is not about rules or ritual or religion. Christianity is not about how to make you more spiritual, but how to make you more fully human. That walking with Christ is not about making you holier, in order that God can love you more and you can love God more. But rather that this exciting process of discipleship (and there is no other phrase for it) is about relationship. It's not our holiness that produces the love of God; it's the love of God for us that produces our holiness.

The exciting thing about God's big picture is that we each have a small part to play in it. We are like the individual component parts of the jigsaw that together go to make up the overarching scene of God's love for His creation. And how do we make sure that our part of the jigsaw fits; that our rough edges are being gradually filed away? Or, to change the image, that we've been cleaned out of any muck we might have brought with us when we were 'born again'? To make sure we carry the life and energy and fun of God and are not stillborn? The only way I've seen in Scripture, the only way I've experienced in my life; the only thing I can pass on to others, is that we grab hold of all this through the process of radical discipleship. This book is an attempt to put to death the lie that to become a Christian, to be 'born again', is to automatically be a 'disciple'. Not so. Disciples are made not born. Not even 'born again'. So here's a book about making disciples. If you want to enjoy the wide place that God has bought for you, there are paths and boundaries to be explored. You can learn to walk the walk, to follow the Way. So, first and foremost, I've written to help you see the extent of life with God.

Secondly, I have written this book in order that once you have established what God has done inside you, you might get what is inside of you out. That you might not just believe it;

that you might not just believe it and talk it; but that you might walk it too. This is how it was meant to be. Not rules, regulations and ritual working their way from the outside into us. Rather the love and life of God working from the inside out of us. You can't give away what you haven't got, but if you've got it you have to give it. You have a difference to make. You have a destiny to inherit. You have a life to live for Jesus. What is *really* inside of you *must* come out. Let words become lifestyle. Let talk become action.

Pete Gilbert

Chapter 1

WHO *AM* I?

Seven of the twenty-six years that I have been working as an evangelist were spent in the East End of London. One evening an incident occurred which over the years I have found myself going back to, as it graphically illustrates to me a reality of how we live our lives.

A friend of a friend was appearing at the Royal Albert Hall. A full dress rehearsal was scheduled for the Friday evening before the Saturday opening. Every member of the cast had been given free dress rehearsal tickets and one of these generously made its way in my direction!

Armed with the ticket, I took the tube from Leyton Underground station to South Kensington and from there to the pavement outside the Royal Albert Hall via the subway. It was a cold and dank November evening and between my getting onto the tube and emerging at the Royal Albert Hall it had also grown misty. The scene was set like something out of a Stephen King horror film!

As I walked along the pavement I could now and again hear, coming out of the mist, the distant echo of the footsteps of infrequent passers-by. As I approached the Royal Albert

Hall, I began to circumnavigate the huge building looking for the correct entrance door, as marked on my ticket. This search eventually brought me near to the main entrances, opposite the Royal Albert Memorial and alongside a set of metal billboards advertising what was to take place at the Albert Hall in the coming weeks. It was as I walked past the billboards, which stood some six feet high and were raised from the pavement on metal legs, that I first heard the sound.

Emanating from somewhere nearby was a low ferocious growling noise. A little spooked by the ambience of the dark, misty November night, I swallowed hard and looked around to see if I could see the dog. Although there was no dog to be seen anywhere, the growling continued and indeed increased in volume.

Then, on looking across to the posters, I realised that standing behind them was what appeared to be (for I could only see him from the knees down) a tall figure wrapped in a long cloak! It was at this point that the full and frightening absurdity of the situation hit me; there was a man hiding behind the posters, wrapped in a long black cloak, growling at me!

Trying to appear cool and nonchalant, I walked on past the posters and then, at the last moment, swung round quickly to see if I could get a better view of this figure. At precisely this moment the figure slowly wrapped one hand around the edge of the posters and peered out at me.

Having first noticed the hand, it was as my eyes travelled slowly from it to the face now peering at me that I registered a chilling fact. The hand had six fingers! Not only that, but it was covered in long matted dark hair, complete with warts and broken jagged pointed fingernails. As I looked from the hand up to the face, reality dawned on me. I was looking into the face of a werewolf!

There was no doubt as to what was peering out at me, and being really rather cool, I did exactly what you probably would have done under the circumstances, I ran!

I must have been halfway round the Royal Albert Hall (I was fit in those days!) before I realised what was going on sufficiently to gather my wits and, panting, stopped running. Some idiot had got himself a monster glove, werewolf mask and long cloak and was standing behind the posters at the Royal Albert Hall growling and trying to frighten passers-by. Which of course in my case hadn't worked! Actually, at the time of this incident there was a spate of such events on housing estates across London, which in a now calmer frame of mind I connected to what I had just seen.

Silly (though true) as that illustration is, it has hammered home for me ever since a reality about the way in which I can live my life, and I don't think I differ from you in this. We can all too readily go through life wearing masks. We adapt the mask to suit the situation or the people we are with, but mask-wearing has become a part of everyday life.

I recently took my wife on a surprise night out to the Mayflower Theatre in Southampton, where we saw a stunning production of Lloyd Webber's *Phantom of the Opera*. If you have ever seen it or any of the films the original book has spawned you will know that it is the story of a man who cannot come to terms with the passions that rage within him, with his love for a woman and for music. This is the story of a man who hates what he is like on the inside as well as what he looks like on the outside and who also fears what others will think of him. Consequently, for 99 per cent of the production, he wears a mask.

TYING GOD'S HANDS

I am gradually discovering that one of the reasons why Jesus died for me was to demonstrate that God Himself had faced the very worst about me, yet still loves me enough to have sacrificed His Son for me. This Gospel of Freedom means that I can also face the worst about myself, without self-loathing and self-rejection. I could even dare to let others in on the secrets; because Christ died for them too.

But what I cannot do, and should not try to do, is to fool myself and other people about who I am and what I am really like. I have come to discover that radical holiness demands radical honesty. Honesty before God and others too; about myself, the kind of person I am, what makes me the way that I am, my hopes and dreams, my fears and sins, my aspirations, my successes and failures. Only pretend to be something you're not and you have immediately entered the realm of religion. Lack of honesty lays the foundation stones on which whitewashed sepulchres are built. The religious Pharisees were like this, and Jesus told them so (Matt. 23). Lack of honesty with and about yourself on the inside eventually will show up on the outside as hypocrisy. You will think one thing on the inside, but say another on the outside; you will believe one thing on the inside, but do another on the outside. And to wear a mask of pretence is to tie the hands of God Himself. He will not deal with the areas we will not yield to Him in honesty and humility. Indeed eventually in these areas He will oppose us (Prov. 3:34 quoted in 1 Pet. 5:5 and James 4:6).

WHY DO WE DO IT?

I have discovered that there are three reasons why we wear masks.

Firstly, we can wear a mask because although that which is underneath is wrong, secretly we like it. The aim of such mask wearing is to deceive. Ultimately, this is a mask of sin.

Secondly, we can wear a mask because we do *not* like that which lies beneath it. The aim of such mask-wearing is to protect; we will look further at this in Chapter 3, and ultimately, although such mask-wearing usually involves great pain, it also is a mask of sin, as it is rooted in a fundamental disagreement with God about what He says about us.

Thirdly, we can be mask-wearers because we are ignorant about who we really are. We can be so out of touch with ourselves, our emotions, passions, drives and desires, that we become chameleon-like in our response to others, constantly changing and adapting to fit in with the surroundings. This is not sin, although it often leads to sins of deception, lack of faithfulness and so on. But there is no premium in ignorance.

If you can identify with all three responses, don't worry! It probably means you're normal. It is not uncommon to wear masks for all of these reasons. A classic example from the Bible would be that of David in the Old Testament (2 Sam. 11 and 12). He sins sexually, first in his mind and then in his body, concerning Bathsheba, but hides behind the first mask of kingly righteous anger against injustice, until exposed by the prophet Nathan. Facing up to his sin is a humbling removal of the second mask, a painful process, producing an intense dislike – yet acknowledgement of who he really is (Psa. 51). And who knows but that in all of this there may have been fundamental questions in David that went right to the root of his identity? For here was a king who was the least, the youngest and the roughest amongst his brothers, almost bypassed by his father Jesse (1 Sam. 16). A shepherd boy who fought armoured giants with slingshots. Who perhaps on occasions wore the third mask of the warrior king because he didn't know who else he was.

AND THE ANSWER IS ...?

For David, a part of the answer to the question 'Who am I?' is found in relationship – with God, and with Jonathan. I hope you can see that the question, which is the title of this chapter, is a good one to ask yourself. Moses asks the same fundamental question 'Who *am* I?' (Exod. 3:11) at the outset of his encounter with God. We would do well to do the same – and to unpack and understand God's answer to this most fundamental of questions. For God's answer to the question 'Who am I?' is 'I will be with you'. In other words, our identity is defined by God's presence with us. Our restless shifting finds its rest in God's unchanging love, hanging out with us. 'I will be [with you]' is the same Hebrew word from the verb '*hayah*' (to be) – that God uses (v.14) to describe His name and nature. 'I AM WHO I AM', always have been/will be, unchanging, unfazed. So where do I discover my identity? I discover it when God is with me. Moses asks the question 'Who am I?' only to discover the ultimate answer: 'God is with me.'

Identity is always seen to be important to God. Adam and Eve are given identities (even names), which reflect their createdness, their relationship with God and their role. They are told to do the same with creation (Gen. 2). We see throughout the Bible that God clearly has a thing about character and identity, often changing people's names in accordance with His working on their identities: Abram, the

exalted father, becomes Abraham, the father of many; S̶ ̶ ̶,̶ ̶.̶.̶.̶
princess, to Sarah, the mother of nations and kings (Gen. 17);
Saul, a Jewish name, to Paul, evangelist to the Gentiles with a
Roman name (Acts 13); Simon, the reed, to Peter, the rock.

'GOD WITH US'

The best example of secure identity in Scripture has to be
Jesus. His name, like God's, is important too. He would be
called Immanuel (Matt. 1:23) which means 'God with us'. Just
as Moses' identity was defined by God being with him, so
ours is defined by Jesus (who is God) being with us. Jesus is
the equivalent name of Joshua meaning 'deliverer of my
people'; and Christ of course means 'God's Anointed One'. So
God's Anointed One delivers you from sin, sickness, suffering,
Satan and the uncertainty of your identity, by being with you:
you find your true identity not in a mask, a relationship, a
possession, a gift, a ministry, the accolade or rejection of
others, but in Jesus. So how important was identity for Him?

I sometimes wonder if we have sold Jesus short on this one.
Historically, we have been so good at defensively propagating
the divinity of Christ, that it seems to me that we have often
forgotten His humanity. Yet the Bible clearly teaches that Jesus
was both fully God *and* fully man. This incarnation was so
radical that by the end of the first century it had already
spawned a number of heresies concerning the identity of
Christ. Some saw Him as switching in some of His reactions
between being divine and being human. Some saw Him as
being simply human, with a divine spark, which was eventually
added to Him. Some viewed fleshly humanity as being so
corrupt that no human being could possibly be divine, and that
therefore Jesus was in fact a kind of divine ghost. But, biblically,

Jesus is the God–Man, fully both at one and the same time.

Self-knowledge must therefore have been very important to Jesus, just as it is for us. Did He know right from birth that He was the Son of God? *Was* eternity in His eyes? Can we agree with the Christmas songwriter that 'the little Lord Jesus no crying He made'? Or, with the Christmas card artists, that He was born with a kind of glowing goldfish bowl around his head! Did the Renaissance painters have it right – that the infant child Jesus could sit upright from birth!

Clearly not! Scripture isn't detailed, but it does indicate that Jesus had to grow in favour, wisdom, obedience and grace (Luke 2:40, 52). Would there have come a time when Jesus faced the very same question, 'Who *am* I?'? How and when did He reach the staggering conclusion of which He later was clearly so aware? Certainly by the age of Bar Mitzvah (Son of the Promise) at 12 going on 13, Jesus seems to know who He is and what He is about.

There is a fascinating insight into His self-knowledge, contained for us in Luke 2:41–50, where Jesus is teaching the teachers of the law and informing His earthly parents that He is about His Father's business. Clearly, by the age of around 30, He is making startling claims concerning His divinity, be that to a lonely and alienated woman at a well in John's Gospel chapter 4, or in a garden in front of 600 or so armed guards a couple of years later, with startling results (John 18). In each case (and there are other examples strewn throughout John's Gospel) Jesus uses a telling Greek phrase '*ego aeme*' to describe Himself as 'I am He'. This phrase is the Greek equivalent of the Hebrew name for God Himself 'Yahweh' (which, as we have seen, comes from the Hebrew verb '*hayah*', meaning 'to be'). So the answer to the question 'Who am I?' was for Jesus the very name of God, which reveals His true identity 'I AM WHO I AM, I am God'. This is why the Jews convicted Him of blasphemy, for which the penalty was death.

Could this emphasis on identity explain why Jesus was at pains to prompt His disciples to explore and understand the importance of the question 'Who am I?' (Matt. 16:13–17)?

Clearly Jesus had answered this question and validates it for us – 'Who am I?' By the time we read John chapter 13, we see that Jesus is sufficiently comfortable with the answer to this question to be able to humble Himself, without feeling threatened or demeaned, and wash His disciples' feet. This is something that only the lowliest servant would have had to do, given the filthy nature of the manure-ridden roads of the day! Yet immediately succeeding this act of humility Jesus acknowledges that His disciples call Him Lord (Boss) and Teacher and calmly says, 'For so I am' (v.13). Jesus is so in touch with His identity and so secure in it that He is able to be selfless. You can only give away what you've got. Jesus' action and statement is thus either schizophrenia personified, ego run wild or the actions of a man who has stared long and hard at the question 'Who am I?' and come to a peace-filled and God-centred answer. How about you?

HOW DOES IT WORK?

A good way to begin to establish and grow secure in our own identity is by recognising those areas from which our identity *is not* derived. We live in an age when the medical profession is constantly urging us towards the values of self-examination; women are to examine their mammary glands and men are to examine their gonads! And all this to avoid the destructive disease of cancer.

But if we are to avoid the destructive disease of rootlessness and uncertain identity, we must equally be prepared for a degree of ruthless (though not introspective) self-examination. May I suggest that you use the list which follows as a do-it-yourself checklist; are any of these the areas from which you derive your primary identity?

Qualifications
Job Status
Ministry Status
Money
Gender
Sexual Preference
Sex
Relationships
Possessions

The list could go on, but these are certainly common traits found in many. Discovering that you obtain a profound sense of identity, a definition of who you are, from any of the above is a good starting place, as it will clearly indicate that your identity is currently misplaced. If as a Christian your identity is not found and rooted in Jesus, then it is not found and rooted anywhere. Jesus came to be with us, to restore our humanity and our dignity, to affirm our identity. Maturity, as a Christian, is based on three great pillars: knowing yourself, knowing God and knowing your enemy.

Jesus had a radical approach to rooting our identity in Him and away from distractions. You can see this evidenced in the story of the rich young ruler (Mark 10:17–31). His identity and a sense of his own value, before God and other people, were firmly rooted in his financial status. The reality was that, in placing his identity in his possessions, the young man had lost who he really was. So he came to Jesus asking how he could appropriate his eternal destiny and, as ever, Jesus' answer was radical. In effect He said 'Remove the distractions. Sell everything that you have and give it away.' This is very much in line with the question Jesus posed on another occasion, 'What good will it be for a man if he gains the whole world, yet forfeits his soul?' (Matt. 16:26). For 'soul' you could legitimately read 'personality' or 'identity'. Or, put in the wise words of martyred missionary Jim Elliot, 'He is no fool who gives what he cannot keep to gain what he cannot lose.'

So, if your identity is to be found rooted in your possessions, you will need to ask some radical questions about who owns what? Do you own your possessions, or do they own you? If they own you, then you would be wise to get rid of them! I had a friend who, during a few months' active rebellion against God, acquired quite a number of trendy possessions, including the latest sound system, CDs, DVDs and so on. When he eventually came back to God, having tried to find his identity in possessions and other people's approval, he heard Jesus tell him clearly what Jesus had told the rich young ruler. Consequently, he and I had a very happy day distributing around his friends in East London some of the possessions that had owned him. The principle is one of nuking the area in which you have illegitimately invested security and identity. If you've built your identity on relationships and on how others view you this doesn't mean that you therefore break off all friendships! Rather it means that you approach your friends now with a degree of honesty and faithfulness, being prepared to lovingly confront them in areas of ungodliness in their lives rather than fearing how they will respond to you. It means letting them in on the struggles you have been going through and going out of your way to serve them in humility rather than looking for ways in which their friendship can bolster your identity. Seeking to establish identity out of friendship, money, kudos and so on, is often a subtle (or not so subtle!) form of power play, which is best combated by a wilful determination on your part to humble yourself – before God does it for you (James 4:6–10).

CLUEDO

Alongside Monopoly, Cluedo must be one of Waddingtons' most popular games. You can get it now on CD–ROM, the board game is still a massive seller and the basic story has been turned into both a film and a TV series. The premise is always the same: you have to guess the identity of a mystery person through a series of clues. It is a matter of asking the right questions, observation and deduction on the basis of evidence presented. Coming to know and understand your own identity is not too dissimilar! I would like to outline a number of clues we can follow in order to get a better picture of who we are, to combat ignorance and masks, and to root our true identity in Christ.

STRENGTHS AND WEAKNESSES

Once you have identified where you have falsely invested security and identity and have begun to radically and actively dis-invest, the use of lists of strengths and weaknesses can be a positive asset in increasing your self-awareness and establishing who you are and what you are currently like. Can I suggest that you format on your computer screen (or on an A4 sheet of paper if that's easier!) two lists side by side. Under the heading of 'Strengths' on the left-hand side write down what you perceive your strengths to be, under the following sub-headings: Physical, Emotional, Mental, Relational, Spiritual. Take your time over this list; most people find it harder to write down their strengths than they do their weaknesses!

Then, in the right-hand column under the heading 'Weaknesses', compile a list using the same sub-headings you used for your strengths.

Now the beauty of this list is that it is entirely subjective and therefore will reflect something of how you view yourself and what *you* perceive your identity to be. The weakness of the list is of course that it is entirely subjective! I would therefore suggest that you find two people whom you trust and count as friends, preferably one of each gender, and do two things: firstly, ask them to compile a similar list concerning you and, secondly, show them your list and ask them to comment more objectively on it. By the way, as it is not unusual for the list of weaknesses to be much longer than the list of strengths I urge you to only spend a few minutes on listing your weaknesses. This kind of checklist may also give you an indication concerning the state of your self-image in which case Chapter 3 hopefully will be a help to you!

One last comment on strengths and weaknesses: it is a wise person who gradually comes to understand that for most of us our strengths are, at one and the same time, also our weaknesses. I am by nature an instinctive person and have learned to listen to my instincts about myself, others and situations around me. This is a strength which, when the Holy Spirit gets hold of it, can become quite prophetic. However, it is also a weakness in that it tends to steer me on occasions away from a more rational approach and towards a more reactive one. Consequently one of my weaknesses is that I can be quite a reactive person, tending to sound off, feeling the need to rant and rave about a situation to get it out of my system, before I can then approach it more calmly! This can be amusing, especially for those who know me well and are prepared to put up with this foible, but I am not proud of it and of course it can be hurtful to others.

Let me use another personal example. I am by nature strong-willed and strong in my opinions and decisive with it! On many occasions this is a great strength and can be combined with one particular style of leadership. However, unless it is countered with good teamwork, and an awareness of my need to listen to others and not barge over them, it can become a weakness, epitomised by dogmatism and dictatorship!

Much of our energy as Christians can be taken up with building safeguards around our weaknesses, avoiding temptations, allowing people to ask us the difficult questions about where we are most prone to fail and so on. And this is all to the good. But in reality the enemy's attack can as often come through our strengths, which we tend to leave unguarded or unanalysed. Let the reader beware!

MIRROR, MIRROR ...

You can take the most commonplace word like 'teapot' and if you only repeat it often enough you will soon become aware of what a strange word it really is! Exactly the same thing can happen with everyday household objects. Take mirrors as an example. Most of the time we take them completely for granted, but if you stop and think about them, or better yet stare into one, you begin to realise how odd and slightly spooky they are! Because the mirror reverses things it is not entirely accurate, yet it remains the best way open to you to get an idea of how others view you. Nonetheless the point is simply made; reflection (which is what a mirror does best!) does aid self-perception. I want to make a plea that reflection, increasingly seen as important to educational processes, is also a vital tool to help you on the road to self-awareness and established identity. Many people of my generation (often loosely termed the 'baby-boomers') have developed highly-motivated lifestyles centred around efficient time-management, the setting and delivery of goals, and are often very driven and achievement orientated. So in my culture there is all too little time to pause and reflect, not only on what has been achieved, but how it has been achieved and what you feel about what has been achieved. This has even become a hallmark of my generation's spirituality, centring, as it often has, around activity and snatched conversations with God en route to doing things for Him.

Forgive the generalisation, but those of you in your twenties or thirties seem to be a generation with more of an emphasis on other values. This is a generation which, by and large, will place higher value on relationship than on achievement. On reflection than on production. This, I think, is a good thing. There is nothing deep or mystical about reflection, it is simply a matter of making space to sit quietly and pick through not only what you have done, but how you did it and how you felt about it. In journeying terms it is about taking in the route and not just steaming ahead for the destination. Reflection, like meditation, is an art which doesn't always come easily, so if you struggle at first – it *is* worth persevering. Of course, there are different personality types and not everyone will get on with all of the processes of reflection. But in my opinion, *all* of us will benefit from *some* measure of it.

THE LEARNING CYCLE

For many of us part of becoming a disciple is about 'learning to learn'. It doesn't necessarily come easily, any more than prayer does, for example. So it would make sense, if we can, to understand better how we learn. I want to outline a tool called the Learning Style Inventory. Again it is only a tool to help you and, like your reflection in a mirror, it may not be entirely accurate but it will increase your perception of how you learn best. There is a note of caution. It would be a mistake for you to seek to grow in self-awareness and self-knowledge *solely* in your preferred style. It would be well worth your while looking to stretch yourself in other learning styles so that you are developing holistically with a three-, rather than a one-dimensional identity!

To help you understand how you learn best you might try to answer the following questions. For each question use the corresponding code:

1 = I am least like this;

2 = I am not very like this;

3 = I sometimes am like this;

4 = I am like this the most.

You need to score each column with a 1, 2, 3 or 4.

STATEMENT	COLUMN 1	COLUMN 2	COLUMN 3	COLUMN 4
a) When I learn	I like to deal with my feelings	I like to watch and listen	I like to think about ideas	I like to be doing things
b) I learn best when	I trust my hunches and feelings	I listen and watch carefully	I rely on logical thinking	I work hard to get things done
c) When I am learning	I have strong feelings and reactions	I am quiet and reserved	I tend to reason things out	I am responsible about things
d) I learn by	Feeling	Watching	Thinking	Doing
e) When I learn	I am open to new experiences	I look at all sides of the issues	I like to analyse things, break them down into parts	I like to try things out
f) When I am learning	I am an intuitive person	I am an observing person	I am a logical person	I am an active person
g) I learn best from	Personal relationships	Observation	Rational theories	A chance to try out and practise
h) When I learn	I feel personally involved in things	I take my time before acting	I like ideas and theories	I like to see results from my work
i) I learn best when	I rely on my feelings	I rely on my observations	I rely on my ideas	I like to see results from my work
j) When I am learning	I am an accepting person	I am a reserved person	I am a rational person	I am a responsible person
k) When I learn	I get involved	I like to observe	I evaluate things	I live to be active
l) I learn best when	I am receptive and open-minded	I am careful	I analyse ideas	I am practical
TOTAL THE SCORES FOR EACH COLUMN				

29

The four columns that you have just totalled relate to the four stages in the Cycle of Learning from Experience. There are four learning modes in this cycle: Concrete Experience (CE); Reflective Observation (RO); Abstract Conceptualism (AC); and Active Experimentation (AE). Enter your total scores from each column:

Column 1 (CE): _____ (Feeling)

Column 2 (RO): _____ (Watching)

Column 3 (AC): _____ (Thinking)

Column 4 (AE): _____ (Doing)

Now in the diagram opposite, put a dot on each of the lines to correspond with your CE, RO, AC, AE scores. Then connect the dots with a line so that you get a kite-like shape. The shape and placement of this kite will show you which learning modes you tend to use most and which you use least.

LEARNING STYLES EVALUATED

Now look at your preferred learning style. There follow some summaries about each one. How well do you feel the following statements describe you?

CE – 'Feeling'
Activists: involve themselves fully in new experiences and like to be involved in activity. They relish coping with crises, are optimistic about anything new and are unlikely to resist

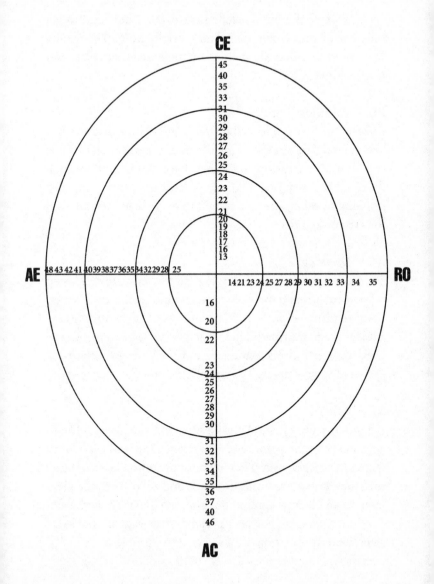

CE

45
40
35
33
31
30
29
28
27
26
25
24
23
22
21
20
19
18
17
16
13

AE   48 43 42 41 40 39 38 37 36 35 34 32 29 28 25

RO   14 21 23 24 25 27 28 29 30 31 32 33 34 35

16
20
22
23
24
25
26
27
28
29
30
31
32
33
34
35
36
37
40
46

AC

change. Once the initial excitement is over they tend to get bored with implementation and consolidation. They enjoy working with others, but tend to do too much themselves and hog the limelight.

RO – 'Watching'

Reflectors: like to collect all the facts and to look at situations from all angles. They are careful and methodical and dislike reaching a conclusion until they have thought it through thoroughly. They prefer to take a back seat, observing and listening to others, but often tend to be too cautious and not to take enough risks.

AC – 'Thinking'

Theorists: approach situations logically, working through step by step, integrating their observations into complex theories. They tend to be perfectionists and reject ideas they see as subjective or intuitive. Their disciplined approach restricts their ability to think creatively and they are unlikely to be prepared to give it a go and see what happens.

AE – 'Doing'

Pragmatists: are practical, businesslike individuals who like to get straight to the point. They are full of ideas and keen to try them out straight away. They are most comfortable with things that they know are going to work and tend to reject ideas without an obvious application. They are impatient with what they see as 'waffle'. If you are a pragmatist, beware of a tendency to seize on the first expedient solution to a problem.

MIXING IT!

Over-reliance on a particular style can become a weakness. If you are equally effective at all stages of the cycle you will increase your potential to learn from all kinds of activities. So deliberately place yourself into situations/experiences that challenge and stretch the way you would naturally prefer to learn. If you're a 'feeler', stop and think, make lists, set goals. If you're a 'do-er' step back a bit, watch others, listen a bit more than you speak, and so on. Mix it around!

DEAR DIARY ...

Many of Jesus' most radical disciples maintained very personal spiritual journals or diaries of their encounters with God. These have come down to us as remarkable insights into the way God works with humanity, but also into the identities and self-understanding of some of the greatest revivalists of our times. The journals of John Wesley and Jonathan Edwards would be good examples. Or, more recently, of Corrie ten Boom. You might even want to argue that the Gospels and some of the Pauline epistles fall into a similar category!

Now, again, I know that some people find it easier to keep journals or diaries than others. I live by my diary as a kind of appointments book (get a life!), but by spiritual journalling I do not mean a kind of retrospective list of engagements! Rather I mean an experiential and emotional analysis of how God encounters you through the little and large of everyday life. Personally I find this quite a daunting challenge and consequently have only kept spiritual journals for specific periods of time often connected to rhythms of great questioning in my life or periods of fasting and spiritual retreats. Whether you do it all the time or you do it for particular rhythms, it is, nonetheless, worth doing.

A FEW TIPS ...

I think that the things to be looking out for are brief records of: what you have done or attempted to do; prayer requests and answers to prayer (great for building faith); hopes and dreams as well as fears and anxieties; how you are currently feeling about God, yourself and others; how you acted and how you reacted in given situations and why you think that was. A spiritual journal is also a good place to write down prophetic words spoken over your life and scriptures that have spoken to you that day. It is also a good vehicle for you to compose prayers, poems, pictures and so on, as God gives them to you during periods of reflection.

I am responsible for a year-long church-based discipleship training programme (called DNA) on behalf of the Pioneer network of churches (although 50 per cent of those on the course come from outside the Pioneer network). All of our trainees are required to keep such a journal. I know many who in years subsequent to completing the course have read and re-read their journal and been astounded at the principles that God has taught them and the revelations about their own identities. It is not uncommon eventually to see recurrent themes, both positive and negative, emerge from such spiritual journalling, which otherwise in the hurly-burly of our everyday lives might go unnoticed. Would you give it a try and see what you think?

NEWTON'S CRADLE

Have you ever see one of these contraptions? I am sure we used to have one at the physics lab at school and certainly you can get them as a kind of executive toy. They normally consist of a metal or wooden rectangular frame from which is suspended, usually on wire or string, five heavy metal spheres. If you raise one at one end and let it go, the imputed force on the line of balls will knock the final one flying into space until it reciprocates and the motion is reversed. If you raise two then two are knocked off and so on. Newton's Cradle aptly demonstrates that for every force there is an equal and opposite force. But human beings, of course, are not so orderly as Newton's Cradle! The principle of action and reaction certainly still holds, but it would be fair to say that where you and I are concerned, actions sometimes produce reactions which are out of all proportion to their cause!

It is for this reason that wise individuals coming to understand themselves and their identity, will realise that they are likely to learn more about themselves from their *re*actions than they are from their actions. Of course, our actions may say much about us, our personalities and our choices. We may *call* ourselves compassionate, but if we fail to choose to do the compassionate thing, the words are meaningless. Actions *do* speak louder than words. But the point is that our actions are choices determined by what we believe to be right or what we would like others to think of us. On the other hand our reactions are often involuntary and therefore have the potential of giving us a disarmingly frank insight into the real you and me!

Actions speak louder than words, but reactions speak louder still! So if I choose to say that I have forgiven someone, but my reaction on being asked to pray for them is that I can't or won't, the chances are my reaction indicates the reality of the situation – I haven't really forgiven them. I may choose to be smilingly gracious concerning my mother's attempts to help our family clear our dining-table, but when she drops a stack of matching plates and they smash, my irritable reaction says more about the reality of my material possessiveness and lack of grace than my former choices do, and so it goes! Please be prepared then to be ruthless in owning and reflecting on your reactions and not just on your actions – they will often give the game away concerning your true identity!

RULING PASSIONS

It is worth making sure that you are in touch with what drives and impels you both for good and for ill. What are your ruling passions? What motivates you when nothing else would? What picks you up when you are feeling down? To what do you turn for comfort and security when you are feeling disappointed, disillusioned or insecure? What really buzzes you for Jesus? How do you most like to be used by Him? What would you most like God and others to say about you at your funeral? What would you want written on your gravestone? These are not morbid but, rather, salient questions to grapple with. Who are your closest friends – why do you like them and why do they like you? Who are your worst enemies – why do you not get on with them, or they with you? We tend to be attracted to people for one or more of the following three reasons. Firstly, because we see something in them that we really esteem and like. Secondly, because we see something in them which is similar to ourselves or, thirdly, because we see something in them which is very dissimilar to ourselves, which we would like to emulate if possible, but which through the proximity of friendship we somehow feel would make us a more whole person.

I haven't just flung out all the above questions. Before we move on to the next chapter can I urge you to sit down and answer them specifically one by one prayerfully and then in consultation with a couple of close friends?

Chapter 2

HOW COME?

'NO MAN IS AN ISLAND ...'

It was the poet and Christian, John Donne, who wrote those words 'No man is an island', asserting that we were each connected to the other, and that none could stand in isolation. Before going on to offer further exercises/tools to aid your self-knowledge it might be helpful to recognise that self-knowledge and self-understanding are *not* the same as self-absorption. Greater self-understanding increases your capacity to give yourself away to others. At the same time your identity was not formulated in a vacuum. Perhaps we need to take a little diversion into some of the background shapers and influencers of our identity.

Your identity has thus far in part been shaped by your DNA, by electro-chemical reactions in your brain, by your personality, your character choices, your upbringing, your conscience, your environment, the culture and social mores. We shouldn't underestimate the extent to which we start off as a product of our past, any more than we should imagine that we are stuck with that like some kind of victim. The reality is that Christ re-routes our identity in Him, but we would be fools not to understand the impact of peer and cultural pressure. So a brief look at some of those pressures might help us now. And if this kind of background is your kind of thing, I've put enough ideas in the next few pages to stimulate your thinking to further reading/research.

GOING WITH THE FLOW?

The reality is that none of us come to know ourselves or indeed are able to answer the question 'Who am I?' in a vacuum. Culture and peer group pressure exerts external forces upon us, causing us to conform and fit into the society around us. Or, for some, to find our true identity in active rebellion against it.

Although simplistic, it might be helpful for us to understand the vast cultural changes that have been taking place to produce this current generation, so often referred to as 'baby-busters'. Up to the eighteenth century (pre-modern), certainly the Western worldview was largely Christian in its thinking and influence. Then from the eighteenth century to around the 1970s (Modernism) the influence of secularisation and humanism was predominant. But in this generation from the 1970s to today (post-modernism) the predominant driving influence has been that of relativism. The idea of the overarching big picture (the meta-narrative) is now seen as defunct. Truth is relative, experience is vital, absolutes and institutions are defunct. The contrast between that generation and mine is stark. The 'baby-boomers' born between 1945 and the 1970s, are achievement-orientated. They work to clearly set goals and invest heavily into the solutions which science, technology and materialism can provide. 'Baby-boomers' are largely either investors into the systems of politics, authority, education, the judiciary, and so on, or are active rebels against it.

But the 'baby-busters' of Generation XY are very different. Since the 1970s the onslaught of relativism has had a profound effect, producing a sense of rootlessness. Where the 'boomers' place high value in achievement, the 'busters' see relationships and inter-personal skills as all-important. Where the 'boomers' set personal goals by which to measure their achievements, the 'busters' place a much higher emphasis on developing a sense of community and communal experience. The death of the old gods of science, technology and materialism has for the 'busters' produced a profound sense of dis-investment away from these areas, and into the exploration of spirituality. Where the 'baby-boomers' *invested* into or *rebelled* against the major institutions, the 'baby-busters' are by comparison largely *evaders* of them.

Now I am writing this book mainly for people who fit in the flow of Generation XY, born since the 1970s, and probably mostly born in the 1980s. Not that that should stop anyone else reading it, I hope! But if you are of that generation, it is important that you come to understand yourself in that context. You are the antecedents of my generation, which sought to actively dismantle the constraints of absolutes and promote the age of 'free love', which is only now proving to have been extremely costly. You are the searchers for relationship, the seekers after wonder in an age which denies wonder. Forgive my generalisations but they are generally true enough to hold value. Yours is the generation where fashion expresses persona, where style precedes content, where exploring intimacy outside of the context of sexual experimentation is rare, or even at times unthinkable – we no longer 'make love', we simply 'have sex' (or one of the many somewhat derogatory words used)! Intimacy reduced to a physical act. Generation XY; perpetually sexually aroused, yet emotionally numbed. Sexually sated and yet relationally stunted. Searching for friendship and yet fearing rejection. This is your cultural context for finding your true identity.

SPIRITUALITY

And for your generation, the definitions of spiritual identity are also changing. It is important to understand the backdrop against which many of your generation are playing out their search for meaning and awareness, for self-knowledge and identity.

When French sociologist Durkheim made his famous distinction between the sacred and the profane in 1912, he was in reality merely harking back to a much earlier Greek Platonic philosophy, which separated the spiritual from the physical. In an age of reason this dualistic approach to life, which is certainly not that of the Bible, ruled wonder 'off the pitch'. When secularisation is the god of the modern age, spirituality takes a back seat. The biblical and Hebrew approach, however, is that *all* of life is about God, *all* of life is spiritual (Jews even have a prayer for when they first open their bowels in the morning!). It is a Hebrew notion that Jesus came that we might be more fully human; it is a Greek notion that He came that we might be more spiritual! It is a Hebrew notion that the redeemed of Christ will inherit the earth; it is a Greek notion that we will flutter on wings and go to heaven! Many Christians have been left with more of a Greek than a Hebrew gospel, and that's not right!

But there is good news. Just as in the nineteenth century the advance of science and the Industrial Revolution led to a spiritual reaction epitomised in the 1870s with the advent of spiritualism, and in the 1890s with the development of such cults as Theosophy, so, too, in the age of 'unreason' we are seeing a reaction. There *is* a new focus on spirituality. Since the 1970s there has been a massive influence on Western thinking by Eastern philosophies and religions. The 1980s saw the dawn of the New Age; in a Christianised era we found ourselves in God, but now gods were to be found in us! We had moved from the age of Pisces (the fish which swims in water) to the age of Aquarius (now we ourselves are the water bearers). Despite the work of such famous atheists as Bertrand Russell, Karl Marx, Aldous Huxley, Richard Dawkins and others, promoting secular humanism, the reality is that spirituality is fast on the increase and can be evidenced every night on the TV in a variety of advertisements; ranging from alcoholic drinks which release life to cars which define personality!

In the nineteenth century Nietzche had wanted to argue that God and morality were simply a means of power play. Marx went along with this: religion is the opium of the people, to dull their pain and keep them 'under the influence' of their 'class lords'. Subsequently, Jung and Feurbach proposed that in reality God was simply a projection of the individual's self! The gurus who underpin the popularist marketplace of Generation XY's spirituality have taken this idea a step further. You can clearly see this progression; US author Thomas Moore, for example, writes much on the 'inner self, balance, creativity, the soul, depth, tranquillity, mystery, self-analysis' without accepting blame and the concept of relative morality. From Jung onwards the culture of our spirituality has been heavily affected by a search for a mythology-which-fits-the-individual, as opposed to a revealed truth. Mythology can be rich in depth and symbolism, but is and always has been hopeless for producing and maintaining public and personal morality. The spirituality of your generation has been largely looking for a universal harmony of nature. You start to see this emerge in the 1970s in a book like *Gaia* by Lovelock.

LIFE IN THE OVERLAP

But the good news for you as a Christian is that maybe now, more than ever before, there is a long way you can 'go with the flow' concerning post-modern spirituality. We have a lot of ground in common. Conservative evangelicalism with its tendency towards defensiveness, exclusivity, confrontation and denigration of experience may have little to offer your generation. But New Testament Judaeo-Christian experiential charismatic Christianity has much to offer. For it is here that we discover a Christianity that is rooted in history, and your generation needs roots. Which does have a sense of wonder, and your generation is looking for wonder. Which is dealing with reality, and your generation is weary of hypocrisy. Where the presence of the *shekinah* glory of God (Psa. 18:12; 104:1–2; Isa. 6:3; John 1:14) can be both known and experienced, and your generation wants to experience life. Word *and* Spirit based Christianity will promote creation care; in Genesis 2:15 humanity is to watch, protect and tend creation (Hebrew word: *Samar*), and to work with, serve and use creatively that which God has made (Hebrew word: *Abad*). Eden is real and the earth will be new (Isa. 60; Rev. 21) and the gospel offers corporate as well as personal hope to the Generation XY'ers.

If you want to truly understand yourself, then I suggest you need to grapple with these major swings in the culture of spirituality, because you don't exist in a vacuum.

GETTING IN TOUCH

Enough of a diversion into culture and context. How to press further into self-knowledge? Well, I think that we often assume that we know automatically what things in life are really important to us. Yet the demands of everyday living may place us in situations where we give little time or reflection, energy or thought to understanding our priorities and our passions. Can I suggest that you embark on the following exercise and use it as a tool to help you better understand yourself and those things that are important to you?

First of all jot down on a piece of paper the five things in life that you would stand up for, that you would be prepared to make a sacrifice over or which, if threatened, you would pay the most for. What five things do you value most in life?

Then try answering the following questions:

- What would you do if you inherited a million pounds tomorrow?
- How would you spend your time if you learned tomorrow that you only had six months left to live, albeit quality time?
- Jot down something that you have always wanted to do, but haven't because you have been afraid to attempt it.
- If you had a fairy godmother who could grant you one wish what would you wish for if you knew that you couldn't fail?

Use these questions as focuses to help you understand your passions and priorities. Looking back over your life so far, can you identify the kind of things, the kind of areas, which made you feel best about yourself? What made you feel good and increased your self-esteem or gave you a feeling of importance? Try writing that down as well.

REFLECTING BACK

What are the events that you think have had a major impact on you and how much influence do you think they have had on your life, your career, your relationships, your identity? Looking back at the path we have trodden can be of benefit in understanding the things which have shaped us and can help us in making decisions about the routes we are to take that lie ahead. These paths in turn will continue to develop and shape us, remembering that our identity is not fixed and immutable!

A good way to approach this is to begin to think of activities, events and experiences to do with your personal and family life, but at this point excluding your social life. Try to include good and bad times, enjoyable or disappointing events or experiences, successes and failures, and then make a list of at least nine high points and six low points. You could even plot them on a kind of chart indicating a level of satisfaction with each event. The chart would look like this:

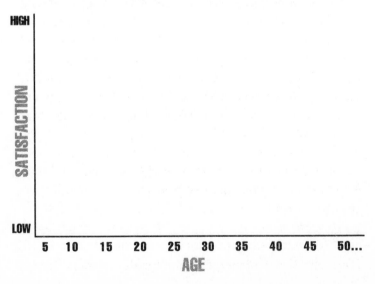

Now repeat the same exercise for activities in your social life, which will probably include friends, neighbours, acquaintances and people you have met in the general course of life. It does not, however, include activities connected to your education or your employment.

Now do the same thing for activities which centre on your education, eg primary, secondary, college, business school, university, postgraduate, correspondence courses, and so on. Try to think too of the people who influenced you or participated with you.

Then, finally, repeat the exercise one last time, but now focused on your employment, if you have already reached those dizzy heights! Start with your earliest efforts to earn income including early 'entrepreneurial' efforts (eg paper rounds, summer holiday jobs, Saturday jobs). Then continue on with your first 'real' job and reflect on the positions that you have occupied since then. Obviously part of these memories will also include the people who were involved with you – such as colleagues and bosses.

The main purpose of this exercise is to help you understand better the sum of experiences which have gone in to make you who you are, both positive and negative. It may, however, be useful in helping you plan for the future, looking for things to avoid where that is in your power, or things to activate where you are able to do so. But the most important thing is the extent to which it informs your self-identity. I guess with increased knowledge we start to move from the question, '*Who am I?*' towards the question, '*Why am I?*'

TRENDY?

Most of us can identify certain trends or traits in our

personality which help to answer the question 'What am I like?' Again, self-understanding is important here but so too is the perception of others. It was the Scottish poet Robert Burns, who said:

Oh, the gift that God would gae us,
To see ourselves as others see us.

The next tool which I would like to put into your hands will help you both self-assess and understand other people's perception of your personality trends. Because we are often quite different in the home environment and in the work environment, I suggest that you do this with the help of both a close friend and a trusted work colleague.

First I suggest that you assess yourself against each trait using a scale of 0–10, where 10 would describe you very well and 0 would describe you very badly. Once you have gone through the entire list go back over the list, adding a plus sign for those traits you would like to increase and be more like, and a minus sign for those you would like to decrease and be less like. It doesn't matter how many of these you mark or how many you leave blank. (See Personality Trait Table, on pages 49–50.)

Then it would be helpful to get your friend and your work colleague to do the same, but in each case ask both to underline the six traits they most value in you. These, of course, may not necessarily be the traits with the highest scores.

TRAIT	SELF-ASSESSMENT	FRIEND-ASSESSMENT	COLLEAGUE-ASSESSMENT
Adaptable			
Adventurous			
Aggressive			
Overt			
Ambitious			
Analytical			
Argumentative			
Artistic			
Assertive			
Boastful			
Calm			
Caring			
Cautious			
Competitive			
Confident			
Conscientious			
Co-operative			
Creative			
Curious			
Decisive			
Dependable			
Diplomatic			
Dominant			
Dynamic			
Easy-going			
Efficient			
Empathetic			
Enterprising			
Energetic			
Enthusiastic			
Extrovert			
Firm			
Flexible			
Fussy			
Generous			
Good Judgement			
Humorous			
Idealistic			
Imaginative			
Introvert			

continued >>

WALK THE WALK

TRAIT	SELF-ASSESSMENT	FRIEND-ASSESSMENT	COLLEAGUE-ASSESSMENT
Intuitive			
Leader			
Loyal			
Mechanically inclined			
Moody			
Open-minded			
Opportunistic			
Optimistic			
Organised			
Outspoken			
Patient			
Philosophical			
Physically active			
Polite			
Punctual			
Practical			
Persevering			
Quick minded			
Relaxed			
Reserved			
Resourceful			
Sarcastic			
Self-controlled			
Self-starter			
Sensitive			
Serious			
Sincere			
Single-minded			
Strong			
Sympathetic			
Systematic			
Tactful			
Talkative			
Tenacious			
Tidy			
Tolerant			
Tough			
Thorough			
Thrusting			
Versatile			

WHERE'S IT HEADING?

You are now in a position to list the six traits you value most highly and the six identified by your friend and your colleague. If you reflect on those three lists you should find that the differences tell you something about the way you are perceived.

How accurately do you really perceive yourself? Can you be encouraged by your friend/colleague's valued traits in you? How about making a more conscious effort in your relationships to develop/demonstrate these traits – build on your strengths. And how about praying into and asking for help and ongoing evaluation in those areas that didn't rate so hot?

You can also use the list developmentally by identifying up to six traits that you most want to feature in your personal and your working life. Self-knowledge is not an end in itself, it is a means towards self-development; just as becoming a Christian is not the end of the journey, but rather the start of one, as we become more like Christ.

THE PRICE IS RIGHT

I think it is true to say that part of the problem of my generation (the baby-boomers) is that we came to understand the *price* of everything, but the *value* of nothing. Fortunately Generation XY is much more prone to examine values, which are ultimately guiding principles that help generate motivation, interest, desire and attitude. If you come to understand your own values you are in a better place to define what it is you want to give to and what you want to get from your environment at both a personal and functional level. Because self-identity and self-knowledge help you understand *why* you choose certain conditions, relationships, jobs and so on over and above others, it becomes easier to place yourself in the best environment for you to give and receive. This will also help you change aspects of your current environment, relationships ... This way you can serve and focus on others better; self-identity and knowledge *isn't* about getting the easiest and best life for you! Try marking on a continuum how strongly you feel the importance of the following values are to you. You can do this exercise both for personal values and then again for career values, if it helps you understand yourself better.

PERSONAL VALUES

Put an X along the dotted line to indicate how highly you rate each statement.

	HIGH	MEDIUM	LOW
FINANCIAL GAIN: The need to make sufficient money to support the lifestyle I want			
PRESTIGE: The need to have high standing or estimation in the eyes of others			
STATUS: Your position/rank in the community			
RECOGNITION: Your desire for public acknowledgement for personal achievements			
AUTONOMY: Desired independence from family obligation			

	HIGH	**MEDIUM**	**LOW**

ADVANCEMENT:
The need for continually improving
status in the community

AUTHORITY:
Having the power to make
decisions for family or direct
community affairs

AFFILIATION:
The need to belong to a family
and/or social group

STRUCTURE:
The need to clearly understand the
responsibilities that are part of your
family or community roles

HELPING OTHERS:
A desire for an opportunity to be
an active member of a service, club,
community group or help other
people in community

VARIETY:
The need for frequent changes in
work responsibilities or locations

CHALLENGE:
An involvement in work that makes
physical or mental demands on you
and which is stimulating work

FULFILMENT:
A strong desire for the satisfying
feeling achieved by completing
work that contributes to the success
of a business activity or the
betterment of society

JOB VALUES

	HIGH	MEDIUM	LOW
FINANCIAL GAIN: The desire for continual increase in pay or salary level			
PRESTIGE: The need for high standing or estimation in the eyes of others			
STATUS: A desire for position or rank in relation to others			
RECOGNITION: The public acknowledgement for achievements			
AUTONOMY: Independence from direction			
ADVANCEMENT: Opportunity for promotion to positions of more responsibility			
AUTHORITY: The need for power to control the outworked activity of others			
AFFILIATION: A strong desire for acceptance as a member of a workgroup or organisation			
STRUCTURE: The availability of clearly defined requirements and relationships			
HELPING OTHERS: Performing work as a service to others			

	HIGH	**MEDIUM**	**LOW**
VARIETY: The need for frequent changes in work responsibilities or locations			

	HIGH	**MEDIUM**	**LOW**
CHALLENGE: Involvement in work that makes physical or mental demands on you, work which is stimulating			

	HIGH	**MEDIUM**	**LOW**
FULFILMENT: The satisfying feeling achieved by completing work that contributes to the success of a business activity or the betterment of society			

You might find it helpful to summarise your personal and job values by placing them side by side according to whether they rated high, medium or low, as indicated below:

Personal Values	**Job Values**
High	High
Medium	Medium
Low	Low

Finally, without a lot of time for in-depth reflection (we are after an instinctive, passionate response here, not a rationalised one!) why don't you try jotting down, in under a minute, the three most important goals in your life right now. How do they correlate to some of the answers to the questions you have answered so far?

ACHIEVEMENTS

Let's take this a step further. I am going to ask you to try do something which most people struggle to do – at least initially. On a sheet of paper try jotting down a description of 30 achievements from your life so far. These are achievements which are of value to you in that they give you a sense of personal satisfaction. Other people may not consider them to be achievements, but that is not the point. For each achievement that you list, jot down what you did and why it gave you a sense of satisfaction. The *why* is as important as the *what* in understanding yourself. If you like, these form part of your previously accrued capital investment in the bank account of your self-worth! The next thing I would like to ask you to do is to look forward to where you would like to invest in the future.

Imagine in the areas I list below that you have already achieved your ultimate dreams, and then try composing a letter to a friend describing how you are now living, under those dream circumstances. Be prepared to let your imagination flow free and don't just put in outline comments, but more detailed descriptions. For example: How much are you earning? What does the nature of your job entail? How many members are there in your family? Or describe your ideal home, for example. In this exercise you are the determiner as to what the precise definition of the categories involves – let it mean to you what you would like it to mean (and if that doesn't sound post-modernistic, I don't know what does)!

> Money
> Career
> Family
> Travel
> Home
> Self-development
> Involvement in the community
> Friendships
> Leisure
> How I spend my time?

PULL YOURSELF TOGETHER!

This is all part of drawing up a portfolio of self-understanding and identity. As you have worked your way through these first two chapters and especially if you have actually embarked on the exercises I have suggested, you should now be in a position to pull together the different areas that we have explored. You could broadly group these together under the headings: 'Who I want to be' and 'What I want to do'. It is important to get these in balance and in the right order since we are primarily called by God to be human *be*ings and not human '*do*ings'! So first try filling in the following summary sheet.

In knowing myself I want in my personal life (*be*ing):

To use the following personal skills

To build on these personality traits

To use these technical skills

To work towards these values

To be involved in these activities

To live in these places

To be with people who are

To pursue these interests

To work towards these goals

And in knowing myself I want in my 'job' life (*do*ing):

To use the following personal skills

To build on these personality traits

To use these technical skills

To work towards these values

To be involved in these activities/functions

To work in this environment

To be with people who are

To pursue these interests

To work towards these goals

AND, FINALLY ...

At the end of these two chapters on self-identity and knowledge, and before moving on to look at self-image, it is worth a final pause to think again on how all of this worked for Jesus. As we have already discovered, the Bible indicates that for Jesus there was a process of growth into self-knowledge and identity, and if you look at the text in Luke 2:40,52, I think we get some key words connected with that process.

WISDOM

Jesus grew in wisdom. A couple of thoughts on wisdom: Firstly, wisdom can be, but is not necessarily, linked to age; you can acquire wisdom beyond your years.

Secondly, wisdom can clearly be given to you as a gift from God and it seems from the Bible that He is pleased to do so. When Solomon asked God for wisdom, God was pleased and granted his request. Solomon could have asked for longevity, power, wealth, but instead he asked for wisdom and God gave it. This is very much in line with the teaching in the New Testament, found in James 1:5–6, where we are told that if we lack wisdom we should ask for it in faith and God will give it to us.

Thirdly, the Bible teaches that the fear of the Lord is the beginning of wisdom (Prov. 14:16) and so as you work through these two chapters I would urge you to bring all of it into the presence of God and to soak all of it, including the exercises, in prayer and meditation. Invite God in on your perceptions and your misconceptions.

Fourthly, there is some textual justification for saying that men and women in the Old Testament who operated under wisdom were operating under the Old Testament equivalent of the influence of the Holy Spirit. You and I are really only wise when we are filled with the wisdom and Spirit of God, and true self-knowledge only comes into proper perspective when it is put alongside an increasing knowledge of God and His Holy Spirit (1 Cor. 2:4–16).

GRACE

Jesus grew in grace. The common acronym for explaining grace is that it is God's Riches At Christ's Expense. The concept of grace goes right to the heart of the gospel of Jesus Christ; it is not a gospel of works. It is not something we earn. We cannot by our actions, or even by the inward changes the Holy Spirit makes in us with our co-operation, somehow acquire more of the love of God. The love of God for you is complete as it stands. It was blood-bought for you at Christ's expense. You are blessed by God *not* on the basis of your deserving, but rather on the basis of His desiring. It is the grace of God in our lives that stops us being driven and yet enables us to fulfil our calling, both in terms of who we are and in terms of what we do. To grow in grace is to grow in a heart understanding as opposed to a head acknowledgement of just how loved and accepted we are. It is the grace of God which allows us to face fully our shortcomings without a sense of condemnation. I would urge you to seek God with prayer, meditation and fasting (Chapter 10 might help with this!) for a fuller, deeper understanding of grace in order better to receive and more clearly to understand the self-knowledge that God would give to you. Self-knowledge with grace leads to maturity. Self-knowledge without it can lead to introversion or even self-destructiveness.

But another important aspect of growing in grace is that having received the grace of God we have more of it to give to others. Grace means that we are more likely to be able to receive from them their love, their perceptions and correctives concerning our own self-knowledge and identity. And grace means we will be better able to extend understanding, love, patience and forgiveness to others in their own search for self-knowledge and identity.

STATURE

When Scripture says that Jesus grew in stature I have no doubt it is referring to the fact that He grew in height(!) but more importantly that He also grew in that indefinable, intangible but vital quality, which relates to the esteem in which He was held by others. Stature has something to do with the dignity which we allow the gospel to invest into us; the seriousness with which we take ourselves. The bearing we bring to our consideration and value of others. And the humility with which we are prepared to accept the positive affirmation and esteem of those around us, as well as the dignity, openness and vulnerability with which we accept correction from them ('Faithful are the wounds of a friend' – Prov. 27:6, NKJV).

FAVOUR WITH GOD

This is surely an interesting phrase! Does it mean that there was a time when Jesus did not have God's favour? Does it mean that the more Jesus grew in God's favour the more God liked Him? I think not. Nor do I think that this is true for you and me. Growing in favour with God has more to do with being able to understand that the heart and hand of God is turned towards you – for blessing, healing, wholeness, forgiveness … – rather than away from you. Often the result of realising this is an increase in the sense of intimacy with God, and an increase in the experience of living in answered prayer, which can superficially give the appearance of God's favour being more towards you. But in reality it's more to do with you and me *receiving* more of the love of God, and therefore engendering a deeper relationship with Him, than to do with God *giving* more. He can't love you any more than He does already. Your identity has already been historically established in Christ (Col. 1:27: Christ in you, and Col. 1:28, 3:3–4: you in Him).

FAVOUR WITH PEOPLE

Jesus grew in favour with people. We shouldn't equate this to a particular personality style (eg affable, outward looking, extrovert, and so on) but rather to a winsomeness, approach-ability, vulnerability, plus a desire to serve people, which I think are hallmarks of a godly lifestyle and series of choices, rather than simply personality. Knowledge of yourself, your strengths and your weaknesses will be directly enhanced to the extent to which you open up your life to both give to and receive from other people. For this reason, growing in favour with people, as well as with God, is an essential pre-requisite of self-knowledge, and a result of it. The concept of the isolated Christian outside of some kind of community of believers is as unbiblical as the concept of a Christian who loves God but hates his fellow brother in Christ (1 John 4:20).

You should know in conclusion to this chapter that I have gone through all the exercises outlined in it (plus others like the Myers Briggs Evaluation and The Belbin Tests for team role, functional preferences, and so on) in an attempt to grow in my own self-understanding. I would urge you to do likewise if we are to ditch the masks we have so often lived behind. 'Who am I?' and 'Why am I like this?' are two vital questions on the route to radical holiness. The next chapter tackles an equally vital area. For all too often when the mask comes off, what lies underneath is not what we wanted to see.

Chapter 3

'HOW AM I?'

I remember a friend of mine quipping, 'You'd worry a lot less about what people think of you if you realised how seldom they did!' At least I think he was a friend of mine! The reality is that for many of us the issue of how people view us is a critical one. For most people, adolescence runs from around the age of 11 to around the age of 21 or even older! Adolescence is marked by a kind of *angst*; it is a time when every inter-related area of our lives is changing at one and the same time, which never happens again during our lifetime. So during adolescence we are changing in the realm of the physical, the mental, the emotional, the social, the spiritual. This produces a tremendous climate of insecurity. Adolescence (and many of you reading this book will likely fall into the top end of that category) is therefore hallmarked by such questions as, 'Am I an OK person? How do others view me? What do people think about me? What do people say about me when I leave them?'

EXTERNAL PRESSURES

Add to this the external pressures caused by a society which still tends to measure worth by performance, where value often equates to job, and where rampant consumerism robs individuals of their dignity and sells it back to them at the price of the product, and you have a heady mix of potent pressures which work against the development of a healthy self-image.

Even that's not the whole picture. As we have seen, this is a generation where style has largely become more important than substance and ever-increasing emphasis is placed on the outward appearance. There was a time when it was mainly females who were under pressure to conform to the image of the 'body beautiful'. When every billboard, every TV advert, every magazine and newspaper, every Hollywood film and each female recording artist re-emphasised the same message: 'Look like this or you are not acceptable.'

However, with the advent of a more socially enlightened attitude towards women – their role, privileges and respon-sibilities (and there is still a long way to go in that arena) – the emergent 'new man' now finds himself with a similar series of pressures to face. It is as likely to be a trim 'six pack' staring at you from the billboarding as a set of mammary glands! A popular tabloid newspaper recently ran a photo competition entitled 'Lunch Pack of the Week!' as a direct counterbalance to some of their rivals' approaches to topless models. For years pornography and advertising have exploited the 'ideal' female form and provoked negative self-image as a direct result of invidious comparison. And now 'new man' is under increasing pressure to demonstrate the right ratio from chest to waist to hips, to have the right hairstyle or designer labels, to drink the right lagers and so on. Combined with an increasing un-certainty of what it means in the twenty-first century to be a man and how that role is acceptably defined in an age of political correctness, it is not difficult to see why the roots and effects of a negative self-image are no longer exclusively the domain of females.

Nor should we underestimate the effect of the baby-boomers' permissiveness, as exemplified through the 'swinging sixties', on Generation XY. The buying power of a booming generation, the reaction away from the deprivations of a post-war generation in the fifties, the power of the emerging media and advertising, the startling effects of the contraceptive pill; all had their part to play in major changes in sexual standards, sexual experience and experimentation. The result of that little bit of history is most clearly being felt on this/your generation now. The concept of 'free love' so prevalent in the sixties and seventies has proven not to be free at all. The cost to family life and society in general has been enormous. The erosion of marriage and the breakdown of the family is now impacting your/this generation at *every* level. For example, it is affecting building developments on so-called green or brown land-sites, as more and more people are choosing or being forced to live in singles' accommodation. There are fewer people marrying in the UK now than at any other time in our recorded history. The divorce rate in the UK is currently running at 40 per cent. Statistics indicate that somewhere between 25–33 per cent of all births in the UK are now taking place outside the context of marriage. Every year we are adding at least another 160,000 young people aged 15 upwards to the list of those who will see their family unit breakdown through divorce and separation. There is a phenomenal pool of ugly pain awash in our society and in your/this generation. Often that pain translates itself into issues of identity and self-image. When a marriage fails it is a tragedy for the husband and wife; but it is utterly disastrous for the children. All too often the process for them involves guilt and self-blame. Most children cannot rationalise it away, they simply react as though mum and dad breaking up must somehow be their fault because after all mum and dad are adults, aren't they? And adults get things right!

In the light of all of that, it is little wonder that many are in desperate need of help from God over issues of identity and self-image. Let's look at this further under the three headings of image, self-image and God's image.

IMAGE

I am defining image here as the way that we look on the outside, or the way that we wish we looked on the outside, and the way that we wish to present ourselves to people we meet, and particularly those people who are important to us.

Many fascinating studies have been made about the way that we assess one another on first meeting. Measuring and mapping eye traces seems to indicate that men and women differ in their approach to this; women spend more time focusing on men's faces, their eyes and their mouth, whilst men, having started there then tend to move on to the breast and hip area! Many studies have also been made about the relative importance of various aspects of communication. How much importance do we attach, for example, to the words that a person uses in communicating with us, to the tone of voice in which they speak and to their body language? Research at Bristol University discovered that only 8 per cent of the content of any communication is done through the choice of words, whilst a considerable 35 per cent is delivered through intonation, and a staggering 57 per cent is done (a large part of it subconsciously) through body language! So you see, image really does matter. So much so that most of us probably anxiously feel at some time or another that if we could only see ourselves as others see us then we would probably have our eyes examined!

How comfortable and at ease are you with the way that you present yourself to others on the outside? How do you feel about your image? The wisdom of hindsight is a great gift. 'If only I knew then what I know now', might help us now to deal with some of the hurts of adolescence. But for many of us the scars acquired *then* by a negative self-image can still ache *now*, many years later.

My dad was always 'hairy'. Genetically I have inherited that trait. I suspect that my son will from me. But for me, approaching adolescence at the age of 11 was a nightmare when I first had to start shaving what looked like rather long and wispy pubic hairs from around my Adam's apple! My horror was complete when by the time I was 14, and still enduring the enforced school games regime and communal showers, hair had spread on my body! Now I took a lot of ribbing about that, largely from boys whose only hair was to be seen above their eyebrows. Add to that the fact that until the age of 16 I was overweight. People kept telling me that it was only 'puppy-fat', but it was enough to make me hate the entire canine world! 'If only I'd known then what I know now!' Then I *knew* that I was hairy, because the hairless ones told me so! What I *didn't* know was that the hairless ones *knew* they were hairless! And what's more that those without hair wanted to have it, whilst those with hair wanted to get rid of it! I thought I was too fat (and the truth is I *could* have done with losing some weight), but what I didn't realise was that many of the lads whom I wished to be more like in body shape felt that they looked like stick insects and were desperate to put on weight and muscle tone. Lads at school who were tall wished they were shorter, whilst the smaller guys, despite quips about 'beanpoles', wished in turn that they were taller. Girls with long hair secretly admired those with short, and vice-versa. Those with curly hair wanted it straight, whilst those with straight hair wanted it curled. A girl beginning her menstrual cycle early was in for some serious mickey-taking, but the reality is that those who hadn't, ended up feeling somehow less of a female. Girls whose chests remained flat looked enviously at those who were now suddenly filling bras with something other than crumpled tissue paper. And most guys, from the vantage point of looking down on their bodies, were convinced that every other guy's penis was much longer than his! It seems to be an inherent part of fallen human nature that we don't like what we've got and we want what we haven't got. And that certainly applies to image as much as to possessions.

Perhaps that is why as people come into adolescence and grow through their teens into their early twenties, marketing forces concentrate on extracting the £18 million plus per week spent by teenagers on image-enhancing products (cosmetics, dietary aids, hair products, toiletries …). And that is before you look at the clothing market. Where in all of this emphasis on external image does the committed follower of Jesus Christ draw the line?

GEEKS FOR JESUS?

I don't think we need to draw it as far back as sometimes religion in previous centuries has seemed to dictate! Sometimes the Church has had a strong reaction against image and imagery, as evidenced in the UK by the Protestant Movement against and away from Roman Catholicism and its then prevalent emphasis on icons, idols and images. The Puritanical fervour extended to the individual's image and indeed there are still modern-day sects like the Amish in the USA for whom a plain and sober image is considered essential in their walk with God. Even the vanity of a zip, let alone make-up or a designer label, would be out of the question!

Not a few fundamental evangelicals have also over the years reacted away from make-up and fashion. Let it be noted, however, that you *cannot* react away from 'image'. Ultimately, however you present yourself will be in one image or another. Is it always right/desirable/godly that Christians dress simply/plainly/cheaply? Should the measure of a girl's following of Jesus be directly proportionate to the extent to which she appears frumpy and dowdy? Must a guy's radicality in following Christ extend to nylon jumpers, Crimplene trousers and white socks with sandals? I think not!

JESUS' CULTURE

In Jesus' culture the only people who were noteworthy for their image were the Pharisees. They wore long white robes in an external attempt to command respect (and indeed financial sponsorship) from those around them. As Jesus was quick and clear to point out, what was on the outside with the Pharisees was nothing like what was going on inside (Matt. 23:27–28). Certainly there was nothing remarkable about Jesus' own image and appearance that would cause people either to accept or reject Him (Isa. 53:2). If anything (the details are sketchy), Jesus seems to have dressed rather well for the culture of His day (John 19:23). Of course, there is an exception to every rule and John the Baptist seems to have provided that. He seems to have deliberately dressed in an odd fashion (Mark 1:6) and adopted an odd diet (locust sandwiches!) in order to draw a deliberate and positive analogy that the people and culture of the day would have understood. So the descriptions of John the Baptist ring with echoes of some of the descriptions of some of the Old Testament prophets, especially Elijah. John the Baptist's 'image' provoked positive comparisons with previous men of God whilst at the same time making a negative counterculture statement.

'I'M OK'

If much of image is about communication, then the first step in communicating the good news of Jesus Christ and how He has affected my life and yours is that as Christians we are 'OK' and normal as opposed to odd. And therefore if God can reach us He can reach other people like us. Yet at the same time, for the follower of Jesus, there are two radical differences to the way that we approach the whole issue of image.

Firstly, we are not dependent on our external image to provide us with a positive and internal self-image. Rather, that comes from knowing that our identity is to be found in Jesus.

Secondly, on issues of comparison, materialism, generosity and debt we follow a different (kingdom) set of values. So when it comes to wearing the latest set of designer labels at the expense of being able to give to Third World debt we will have a different set of priorities.

Part of the church of which I was a member for 19 years expresses itself in the form of youth church. A couple of years ago, out of a growing concern about what appeared to be a materialistic approach to image amongst members of the youth church, its leaders suggested a rather unusual fast. The church was invited to fast from all make-up and designer labels over the period of a week, which embraced a Sunday meeting. The fast was as difficult for some of the young people as missing a week's worth of meals would be for others of us! But the point of the fast was the same; are we ruled by our desires or do we rule them? Are we dominated by our image, or does it serve us and others?

SELF-IMAGE

I am using this term to refer to the way that we view ourselves on the inside. Obviously the way that we view how we look, how well we feel we carry clothes or what we can afford to spend on them, what weight and shape we are, the colour of our hair and eyes, the proportion of our bodies, and so on, all affect the way that we feel about ourselves on the inside. But it is important to differentiate between root and fruit. I would suggest that the root of feeling positive about ourselves works from the inside outwards and not from the outside inwards. If you are at peace with yourself about who you are on the inside then ultimately whatever is happening on the outside need *not* affect that peace. I am reminded of the first time I saw the stunning film, *The Elephant Man*, starring John Hurt. It was one of those memorable occasions when at the end of the film (you may remember that it is shot deliberately and entirely in black and white) the entire cinema audience sat in stunned silence as the credits rolled rather than making a dash for the exits. In the film Merrick, as portrayed by John Hurt, when finally cornered by a mob in a public urinal, cries out the telling line, 'I am not an animal. I am a human being.' Despite terrible external deformity the character is portrayed with real depth of integrity and humanity because he is in touch with who the real Joseph Merrick is on the *inside*. This apparently reflected Merrick's real-life personality; he was a man of great compassion, culture and religious feeling.

Real life teaches *us* the same lesson. Have you ever been privileged enough to know someone with some kind of physical infirmity or disability, who either because of or despite that, has come to a place of peace and knowledge concerning his or her true identity in Christ? Over the years I have had the privilege of working with a number of such people and have had to re-evaluate the connection between image and self-image accordingly. It seems to me that whilst a healthy internal self-image can positively affect the way that we present ourselves on the outside (image) it can at the same time stop us going overboard into the arenas of materialism and vanity. I think that I have also realised that no amount of adjusting your outside image can heal a fundamentally damaged internal self-image.

INSIDE OUT?

The reality for all of us is that we all live on the 'inside of ourselves'. Of course there is a connection between how we *appear* to be and how we actually are on the inside. But the way in which we feel about how we appear to be often comes from the way that we feel on the *inside* rather than the other way round. Anorexia is a classic case in point, afflicting as it does both male and female. It doesn't matter how many times you tell anorexics that they have lost weight or are even painfully thin, what matters is how they feel about themselves on the inside, where the issues can have more to do with fear of growing up, rejection of responsibility, seeking the 'sanctuary of the child', self-hatred/loathing/destruction or control and manipulation of circumstances, where in other areas of life there may appear to be no hope of control. No amount of external fashion-orientated image adjustment will deal with this damaged internal self-image.

A negative self-image appears often to be more connected to the way that we feel about the kind of people we *are* rather than the kind of people we *appear* to be. So negative self-image often forms around *our* perceptions of our personality, character and the way we *think* other people do or do not relate to or like us. We might assess our worth or value to be that which our parents, our teachers or our employers (importantly all authority figures in our lives) place on us. We may feel that God ignores or even hates us (the supreme authority figure). Perhaps we have lived with constant disapproval, negative words and comparisons, or have suffered acute rejection (be it in the form of lost friends, broken family or even bereavement). In each case the result may be the same; we may find the seeds of negative self-image sown in the roots of our lives. This is not so much to do with how we *appear*, but with who we feel we *are*, or who we feel other people think we are. Equally, living with guilt, be it real or imagined, whether we are perpetrator or victim, can have a similar effect on our internal self-image. Often we can make misplaced attempts to feed the internal craving we have for acceptance, approval and affirmation, which has been starved by an internal negative self-image. This can account for various forms of self-abuse such as over-indulgence in drinking alcohol, in eating or in starvation, in too much exercise or not enough of it, in insatiable and uncontrollable sexual appetites and in psychological, and even chemical, dependency on smoking, and other drug abuse. Left to our own desires to find comfort or to punish ourselves we are trapped in the cycle of image and self-image and the way in which the latter feeds the former and the former is driven by the latter. It was clinical psychologist Dr

Guido Groeger who commented that 'good self-image is either acquired or it is non-existent'. What we need is for something to break into the circle of image and self-image, to produce an objective perspective on ourselves. This is of course exactly what God has done in providing a view on us, which at one and the same time gives us a healthy respect for our image, making the most of what God has given us, and heals our perspective on our self-image as we come to realise and embrace more fully who we are in Christ.

GOD'S IMAGE

As it says in the book of Proverbs (Prov. 1:7): 'The fear of the LORD is the beginning of knowledge.' The word 'fear' here is a rather negative translation of a healthier and much more positive word in the original Hebrew. If we spoke more about respect and reverence for God we would be closer to the original meaning. It is when we begin to give due weighting and respect to what God has said about us that knowledge, wisdom, clarity and healing comes in the whole area of self-image.

UNIQUELY MADE

The fact of the matter is that you really *do* matter to God. When He made you, He made you unique. The God of the individually crafted snowflake and spider's web, so shaped you and me that from our DNA pattern to our fingerprints, from our brainwave pattern to the formation of the eye's retina, we are uniquely individual. When God made you He took one look at you and threw away the mould! That is not because when He made us it all went horribly pear-shaped, as some of our internal thoughts would sometimes tell us! It is because

God realised in making you and me that He would never be able to improve on that and that the next time He made anyone else He would have to start all over again from scratch. This is the God who knows how many hairs there are on your head and what your clothing and shoe size is (Deut. 8:1–5). This is the God with a painstaking attention to detail, who knows every time a sparrow drops but is infinitely more concerned with you (Matt. 10:29–30). This is the God who, when He had made everything else in all of creation, said it was good, but when He had made people like you and me and then looked at creation He said it was *very* good (Gen. 1:4, 31). This same God has been at pains to record in His Book (sometimes at the cost of the blood of the martyrs), that you and I were known by Him even before we were formed in our mothers' wombs. That when He put us together we were 'fearfully and wonderfully made' (Psa. 139:14), whereas half the time most of us seem to think that we are merely 'fearfully made'! My God and yours describes us as the apple of His eye (Psa. 17:6–9).

UNIQUELY GIFTED

The whole of the Godhead was involved in putting you together and gifting you uniquely. The Father's will was expressed in your creation and as a created being you are uniquely and naturally gifted. It may be that you are gifted with humour, or wisdom, or musical ability, or that you can draw, or act, or have infinite patience with children, or the ability to understand how things work, or to make money, or teach others, and so on. But naturally gifted you will be, because you reflect the Father in His creation of you.

You are also gifted by the Son, who has given you a unique way to serve Him and others, and to reflect Him to others, which no one else can do. This is called your ministry. If you want to know what your ministry is, then first, love Jesus and, then, identify what it is you like doing. Because when you love Jesus your ministry becomes your life. That's why Early Church teacher Augustine could write 'Love God and do as you like'. Your ministry is simply your area of work or service for Jesus and others, and the Son has gifted you in those ways.

You are also gifted by the Holy Spirit with supernatural, spiritual gifts, which go beyond your natural giftedness and enable you even better to serve God and others (Rom. 12:1–8; 1 Cor. 12:4–7; 1 Pet. 4:10–11).

So you see, every part of you really does matter to every part of God. God is *for* you (Rom. 8:31–39). One of the roles of the Holy Spirit is to convince you that you belong to Him and that He is your 'Daddy' (Rom. 8:15–16). God has set in front of you good *days* for you to enjoy (Psa. 139:13–16). He has in His heart and mind for you good *plans* for you to move into (Jer. 29:11). He only has good *gifts* for you and every good *thing* that you have ever experienced came from Him in the first place (Luke 11:13; James 1:17).

SELFISH OR SELFLESS

But surely as a radical follower of Jesus we shouldn't be wrapped up in how we feel about ourselves, we should be selflessly giving it all away? Isn't it narcissistic to bang on about self-image? But this is the point. You *cannot* give away what you do not have. You *have* to receive God's love before you can give it away to others. If you don't matter to yourself you will find it hard to believe that you matter to God, or that you matter to others. You can't love God and other people properly if you constantly undervalue His and their love for you. Nor can you accept other people's faults unless you first accept your own. On the other hand if you learn to love yourself you will find it easier to let others love you. If you have experienced love you will find it easier to love others and to love God. The equation is simple and biblical: Be loved by God and others, therefore love God, yourself and others. Why do we love God? Because He first loved us (1 John 4:19).

In fact this is so biblical it is mentioned seven times in the Old and New Testament combined! Anything mentioned that many times as a command is surely worth taking notice of; it occurs in Leviticus 19:18, Matthew 22:37–39, Mark 12:31, Luke 10:27, Romans 13:9, Galatians 5:14, and James 2:8. Neither the Old Testament nor Jesus said, 'Love your neighbour *instead* of loving yourself.' Rather, it is a double command: 'Love your neighbour. Love yourself.' You and I don't have a biblical option. We are not allowed to hate ourselves and love our neighbour. In fact we are not even *able* to do that – we would probably hate our neighbour as well. Such biblical self-love is the only way in which we can actually be selfless and not selfish. Egoists are selfish precisely because they are trying to fill the void of self. If you don't love yourself in the biblical sense you will actually become selfish, completely wrapped up in yourself, and please believe me, that is a very small parcel! Not to develop a healthy self-image is to fundamentally disagree with God seven times! And if that's not enough, check out the two passing references which promote a biblical, selfless self-love on top of the seven mentioned. You'll find these additional references in 1 Samuel 18:1 and Ephesians 5:28–33.

BUT HOW?

We have already gone some way down this route. The references

I have mentioned above are not attempts to validate what I am arguing, I am not using them as 'proof texts'. Rather they are there in order that you might read them and ask God to really hit you with a few of them. I am quite certain that God will do that since that is how God uses and applies Scripture to us. When He has done His work, it is then down to us to do ours. So, firstly, this means memorising some of these verses (perhaps initially writing them down until they are in our heads and hearts) and then quoting them to ourselves and to the enemy when we are particularly inclined to listen to or act on lies rather than truth about our self-image and identity. Correct Holy Spirit breathed biblical teaching can defuse wrong teaching. The wisdom and the Word of God *is* like a medicine to our bones (Prov. 3:7–8).

Secondly (and I don't write this lightly), to harbour, to accept or even to nurse a negative self-image really is to fundamentally disagree with God's perspective on us. Ultimately, however damaged or wounded we may feel, disagreement with God is rebellion and sin, and requires repentance and agreement with Him. To agree with God and to make a positive confession concerning who we are in Christ will also save us from self-pity. The promise of 1 John 1:9 that God will both forgive us and cleanse us is an important one.

Thirdly, we must get a strong grasp of God's redemptive abilities. Martin Luther hit it on the nail in his Fourth Resolution at Wittenberg when he said, 'God's love does not love that which is worthy of being loved, but it does create that which is worthy of being loved.' What is more, God's love for us is perfect. Finding yourself fearful of rejection, of other people's perceptions of you, of your own perceptions of yourself or even of receiving God's love, can all be dealt with by God's perfect love for YOU – 1 John 4:18 makes it quite clear: fear goes when love grows. It is important to remember that this is a process. That verse is written in the present continuous tense, which states that God's perfect love for you drives out fear on an ongoing basis, as many times as it needs too. Rarely is it a matter of 'I used to be scared of rejection but after a prayer time I'm now fine'! Usually it's a process of taking ground little by little, friendship by friendship, compliment by compliment, prayer by prayer. Fear is connected to punishment, and it takes most of us a while to grasp the grace of God and let it souse us with His love.

So, the Spirit-breathed Word of God will help set us free from a negative self-image. From my own experience and from dealing with the lives of countless others over the years who have suffered, as I have, from a negative self-image, let me finish this chapter by highlighting seven common steps in the process of walking free.

1. IDENTIFY THE CAUSE

It is always better to deal with roots rather than just fruit. For three years we had a diseased cherry tree in our garden. The first four years after we moved into the house, this cherry tree threw out beautiful pink blossoms every spring and filled the garden with a heady scent which promised the forthcoming summer. But some years ago something went wrong with its roots. And that became immediately apparent in the fruit that it bore. First it started bearing rotten fruit and then hardly any fruit at all. But it also poisoned the ground in which it stood, to the extent that we ended up with a circle of mushrooms around the extremities, where the roots underground had died! For three years I continued to try to treat the tree's disease by merely tinkering with the fruit. I pruned it and lopped off bad fruit. I cut it back. I kept plucking up the mushrooms from the garden; but eventually the grass died in the circle around the tree. I put on lawn fertiliser and grass seed. But at the end of the day the roots had gone bad and the tree had to be removed; which eventually I did and now the garden is back to its full health. Don't tolerate 'bad fruit' in your life and keep trying to patch up the poison, instead always go for the roots and get rid of them. Are the roots of your negative self-image to be found in your adolescence; in disapproval and negative words, or even curses spoken over you (in which case you may find Chapters 5 and 6 helpful to you)? Do you carry a constant sense of rejection, as though you are worthy of or 'fated' to be rejected? Do you live with a strong sense of guilt – real or imagined? Is there unconfessed sin in your life? Are you dogged by a sense of drivenness or the need to prove yourself, or are you constantly comparing yourself with others? Identify the cause. Name it. Be ruthless and real.

2. EMBRACE THE IDEAL

Way before you *feel* it to be true, ask God to give you first a glimpse, then a hope and then a desire for *His* ideal perspective on you rather then yours. It is at this level that Holy Spirit breathed biblical teaching starts to kick out negative wrong understanding; you begin to 'see' the truth about yourself, even if at this stage you feel you need binoculars!

3. CONFESS THE NEGATIVE

The only way that sin leaves your body is through your mouth! This means that where you and I have fundamentally disagreed with God about who and what we are, we must confess that to

Him and ask for forgiveness. That forgiveness is readily ours, so this is not a recipe for 'a problem party' or 'a pity pot'.

4. ASK FOR HELP

Remember we said earlier that all discipleship needs a context and that the context of radical discipleship is radical relationships? I have found that you can't learn to love yourself on your own; you have to let others in. It will almost certainly be the case that if you have been disagreeing with God about who and how you are, then you have been agreeing with the enemy about what you are not. Since the enemy is a legalist he will always seek to occupy any ground that you give him. It may be that there are negative 'landing strips' in your life on which the enemy has been coming and going for too long. You will probably need a small circle of close friends to pray *for* you persistently so that as hope and faith grow in you they can hit the right time to pray *with* you. Then, if there are any enemy strongholds in your heart and mind, they can be dealt a deathblow. There is a principle of confessing to one another in order that we might be healed – and sickness can be much more than merely bodily sickness (James 5:16). This is why in the New Testament the word for salvation (*sotereo*) also gets translated as wholeness and as healing, and it's why there are gifts of healing (1 Cor. 12:9), because we can need physical, mental, emotional, relational and spiritual healing.

5. CONFESS THE POSITIVE

As a friend of mine says, 'All expression deepens impression' and where once you were fundamentally disagreeing with God about who and what you are, now is the time to start agreeing with God and confessing this out, both in the form of prayers, and in the form of throwaway comments in conversations with your friends. In other words, in the presence of God and your friends (and indeed your enemies) talk yourself up don't put yourself down. So much more than 'psycho-babble positive thinking', confessing the positive doesn't *create* the positive within you, it acknowledges the positive that God can/has put in you of Himself.

6. BUILD THE RIGHT FRAMEWORK

I can only give examples here because we are all individual and have individual needs, but let me speak from my own experience. The insecurities I had about my identity in part latched on to the way I perceived my weight. The more I felt that I was overweight, the more I didn't like myself. The more I didn't like myself, the less I cared about how I looked (although really on the inside I cared very much). So the less I cared about how I looked, the more I would 'comfort eat', and the less I would exercise. Now part of building the right framework is to start reversing that process. Because I had become more aware of the root causes of my insecurities, because I had embraced God's ideal about who I really am, because I had confessed my sin in disagreeing with God, because I had had repeated and persistent prayer for positive self-image, and against a negative one, and because I now began to confess the positive and to no longer think 'I am an insecure person', but rather 'a person with flashes of insecurity', so too I became more inclined to build a healthy framework. This meant that I began to watch what I ate and when I ate it. It meant that I began to indulge in moderate exercise. It meant that when it came to how I dress I started to pay more attention (with the help of my wife!) to the clothes that I bought and wore, without becoming excessive or materialistic (because I have other priorities). In other words I want to make the best use of what God has given me. Now where is your framework for life shaky or unhealthy? You need to find it and reverse it. Perhaps it is to do with eating. Or exercise. Or clothing. Or how tidy your home is. Or how you shy away from relationships because you are scared of rejection even though you crave people to seek to build a friendship with you, thus proving that they really do care. Perhaps you need to be more careful about how much rest you get (1 Kings 19:4–8). Perhaps you need to be active in talking to your soul and stirring yourself up towards God and others (Psa. 103:1). Whatever it is, rebuild the damaged frameworks.

7. INVITE THE HOLY SPIRIT TO FILL THE FRAMEWORK

None of this is possible without keeping a Godward perspective. We are not dealing here with positive thinking. So Holy Spirit inspired praise and worship will be vital to this process; have a look at Daniel 4:34 and the effect it had on Nebuchadnezzar, or on Saul in 1 Samuel 16:23. Make sure that on a daily basis you are inviting God in on the process and are constantly seeking, as the present continuous tense encourages you to, in Ephesians 5:18, to 'be filled with the Spirit'. Never stop finding things to be grateful to God about. Never fail to acknowledge the paths He's led you on and don't spit on your past.

Finally, I repeat: my experience of all of this is that it is a process. You should find as you grow in positive self-image that your awareness of your identity in Christ and your authority in Him also grows (see Chapters 1 and 2). But every so often you will hit a little glitch. It is as though you have gone so far on the new territory which Jesus is giving you concerning your self-image and identity, but when circumstances change, a relationship ends, or a new one begins, or you find yourself in novel, challenging or threatening circumstances, you may find that you have to find God and yourself all over again in that new place. This is not a retrograde step, rather it is God constantly seeking to extend your boundaries.

As I said earlier, I used to be an insecure person. But now I am a person with flashes of occasional insecurity. I can identify quite often when those flashes of insecurity will occur, because of the circumstances which provoke them. I also know what they feel like and they won't feel much different to what they used to. But they no longer have the same intensity or duration that once they had. They afflict me from outside, they are no longer rooted deep within me. I have learned in this area, having done all else, to '*stand*' (Eph. 6:13). Ultimately, the ferocity of your enemy's attack in the area of your self-image will only be for a season. It is a 'day' of evil (Eph. 6:13). It doesn't have to go on indefinitely.

Why don't you take stock of these last three chapters that you've begun to work through before you go any further. If you want to take following Jesus seriously then I would urge you for your sake and His to outwork what we have covered so far and let the words on the printed page do that vital 18-inch drop from your head to your heart and from there into your experience. Once you have done that come back to me in Chapter 4 where I would like us to explore an issue which has been key in the UK at least since the First World War, but perhaps never more so than right now, for your generation.

Chapter 4

DADDY?

We spent time in the first three chapters carefully unpacking and examining our experiences and our perceptions of ourselves. Hopefully, this process of self-discovery has been revealing some of the values that either underpin or undermine our experience and perceptions, depending on whether our values are positive or negative. The reason we have spent so much time looking at identity and self-image is because our identity in Christ is wrapped up in two core issues and this is the first: 'How do we see ourselves?' The second, which we're now moving on to is: 'How do we see God?' It was the Christian theologian A.W. Tozer who said, 'What first comes into our minds when we think of God is the most important thing about us.' Certainly it is my experience that when the pressure is really on, and we find ourselves facing the toughest of circumstances, we hit something of a watershed in our relationship with God. Dependent on your view and understanding of Him, your experience and perception of Him, under such circumstances you and I will either drive into God if we see Him in a positive light, or run away from Him if we see Him in a negative one. Because of this, and because harbouring a distorted image of God ruins our fulfilment and enjoyment of being a follower of Jesus, the whole question of how we see God becomes a major target for enemy activity in our lives. This I can guarantee – if your image of God is distorted you will never reach your full potential in God. You probably won't even want to.

TITLE OR TRUTH?

Consistently throughout the Bible God is portrayed as the ultimate Boss. This phrase is often lost on us since it is usually translated from the original languages into the word 'Lord'. We can take that to be some kind of mystical or Messianic title, and we can sometimes miss the fact that it is actually more a description of function. It embodies a definition of the nature of our relationship with Him. It is a little like my friend Phil who is based in Molesey – he is a GP and I could correctly refer to him as Dr Moore (although I never do!) but the reality is that he is not a doctor to me, because my doctor lives in Inverness. It is the difference between the mere title and the reality of function. So Scripture presents God to us as the ultimate authority figure. It also presents Him to us as a very particular kind of authority figure; as a Father. But, again, we have to resolve whether this is in title only or in function. We might know that Jesus is called Lord, but never have resolved issues of His Lord/Boss-ship. Or God may be our Boss, but never our Dad. We might *know* in our heads that God is a Father, but never *experience* in our hearts that He is fathering us. If our experience is not that God is the very best Boss that there could ever be to us, and the very closest Father that we could ever have, then we will tend to project on to Him from our experiences of earthly authority figures and fathers. Now this is actually the wrong way round. We are now in danger of merely interpreting Scripture experientially instead of through revelation, which latter affects our experience. We are in danger of thinking that God calls Himself a Father because we have earthly fathers and it will help us understand a bit of what He is like, instead of realising that we have earthly fathers because God is the supreme and perfect Father from whom all fathers and families takes their names (Eph. 3:14–15). The Greek phrase is '*pares patria*', a kind of punning way that Paul uses to describe God as 'the Daddy of all daddies'.

Of course, the role of a mother is just as vital as the father's to the healthy development of a child, and of course, God is neither male nor female, and all maleness and fathering finds its fullness in Him, as does all femaleness and mothering. God created male and female both in His image (Gen. 1:27). It is for this reason that there are significant numbers of female images describing God and His attributes in both the Old and New Testament. One of the very names of God (and, as we have seen, names in the Bible usually denote aspects of character, which is why God often changes people's names when He changes people) literally means 'God the big breasted one'! This refers to His ability to provide, suckle and nurture His children. Jesus was equally unashamed to use female imagery in describing His role and attributes as a part of the Godhead, likening Himself on one occasion to a mother hen! At the risk of oversimplifying, psychologists do sometimes delineate between the role of the mother, which is to provide a sense of well-being, care and protection, affirmation, love and support, and the role of the father, which is to provide a sense of identity and place of 'fit' within the overall scheme of things. Thus a father affirms his daughter in her essential femininity and yet at the same time affirms his son in his essential masculinity. This may in turn go some small way towards explaining why an absent father may often be cited as instrumental in the development of homosexual tendencies in his child's sexual orientation.

Perhaps ultimately the reason why Scripture places more emphasis on the revelation of God as Father, and why Jesus Christ is the Son of God, is because there's a greater need for masculinity to be redeemed and remodelled? Certainly, at the least, God fulfils to His kids the classic male *and* female roles of father *and* mother – there is no sexism in the Godhead! More of this later in Chapters 7 and 8.

SO HOW DO YOU RELATE TO GOD AS A FATHER?

I was fortunate enough to get on very well with my father and am in part a product of my parents' commitment, sacrifice and love. But even if you were somehow to take the very best of all the good parents who have lived in the history of humanity, with every sacrifice made, all the unconditional love given, all the protection, provision and care demonstrated, and put it all together, it would still be only a pale reflection of the fathering of God. God does not share in our fallenness. He is affected by it, hurts over it, got involved with it. Yet because He is sinless and perfect, and we are not, He remains separate from our fallenness, and therefore remains perfect as a Father (Isa. 55:9).

So even when we've had good parenting and a positive role model, it is important to understand that it is OK to admit that our parents didn't get it right all the time, just as the Bible realistically portrays (Heb. 12:7–10). Even with the best will in the world there will have been aspects of your parents' parenting of you which would have even hurt or damaged you, as there was for me, and as there doubtless will be between me and my children. It may be an efficient ego inflator to foster the image that as a father I can do anything, know everything, fix everything and provide anything, but it is bad for reality! And even pre-teen my kids had it sussed that I am not really like that anyway! It is as we are realistic about the limitations of our parenting that we can then learn to extend forgiveness, understand our parents' humanity and move on from there, to be able to truly honour them as they are, not as they might be, as Scripture encourages (Deut. 5:16).

WORSE THAN THAT?

Unfortunately, for many of us, our experience of being fathered is very much worse than that. I mentioned in the last chapter that more than 40 per cent of marriages in the UK now end in divorce; more than 25 per cent of babies born in the UK are now born outside of the institution of marriage. Every year more than 160,000 teenagers will see their families split up before they reach the age of 15. Statistically the chances are that many of you reading this book will find yourselves in such a situation. I have had the privilege of talking and praying with many people whose relationship with their earthly father could best be summed up under one of the five headings below.

Forgive me for generalising, but you might find it helpful to read through these descriptions and maybe even assess the extent to which you feel one or more of them applies to you. Why don't you rate them on a sliding scale, where 5 describes your relationship with your father very accurately and 1 describes the relationship hardly at all. If you find that your overall rating is coming in around the 15 mark or above, chances are you have a lot of adjustment to do in terms of how you see God as Father. Any single rating around 3 or over will need some work done in that specific area to address a wrong perception of God as your Daddy.

ALOOF

The father who is aloof is the father who is distant from his children. It may be that his personality (perhaps due to the way that he himself was parented) is undemonstrative and unemotional. Perhaps he doesn't find it easy or natural or even desirable to hug or cuddle his kids. It may be that his love for you has never been in dispute, you know he loves you, but don't often feel it because it isn't said or demonstrated. It may be that all the time your father's energy and attention has been directed towards providing for you at a financial or material level as a demonstration of his love, rather than at an emotional level as well.

AUTHORITARIAN

This is the Victorian father figure with the mutton-chop whiskers! It is the strict disciplinarian meting out justice and demonstrating fairness more than mercy. It is worth remembering that God is not 'fair' to us. If He were, we would be eternally separated from Him. Rather, He is *merciful* to us. The authoritarian father figure is constantly prodding his children forward with a metaphorical big stick, with a focus on 'could do better' rather than an affirmation of 'did do well'. His children's lives are bound in rules and regulations. With an authoritarian father figure, approval is often *won*, if it is felt at all; it is seldom lavished.

ABSENT

With the numbers of those getting married decreasing and with the numbers of marriages and remarriages breaking up increasing, it is statistically and culturally no surprise that absentee fathers are on the rise. So it may be for you as you read this that the closest you can come to identifying where you stand in relation to being fathered is that you simply *haven't* been. That in your life there is a complete absence of a father figure. It is not necessary even that you come from a broken home for that to be the case. Fathers can be present in body in the family home, yet absent in influence and in fathering. The very passive father who takes no role in parenting his children either positively or negatively will, to all intents and purposes, be absent. My wife and I recently attended a parents' evening at our children's school in order to meet with their teachers individually, to go through their work and assess how well they are settling both academically and socially in their classes. On coming out from the school and getting back into the car we were distressed to see in the car next to us a father sitting behind his steering wheel reading his newspaper, whilst his wife went in to do the 'interface bit' with the teaching staff. Abnegation of responsibility or passivity provides a child with an absent father. So too does the very hard working father, who out of a desire to provide for his family gets his priorities imbalanced. A father who works every hour that God sends in order to prove to his children how much he loves them by providing the latest electronic game, would perhaps be better providing them with more of his time and attention and less of his absence.

ABUSIVE

The jury is still out on whether the cases of child abuse are on the increase in Britain or whether opportunities for reporting and recording them have simply improved. But one thing is clear; the image of a dad for many of us may have suffered severely at the hands of an abusive father. Such abuse can take various forms, be it verbal, emotional, physical or sexual. But in each case it is such an inherent contradiction of the reality of what God is like as a Father that it is extremely destructive of the perpetrator, of the victim, and also of the victim's perception of God.

ACCUSING

The accusing father is often a parent driven by a sense of his own failure or inadequacy, who lives with an abiding sense of 'never having made the grade'. Haunted perhaps by a sense of his own unfulfilled expectations, and weighed down perhaps by the unrealistic expectations of the authority figures in his own life, the accusing father then often repeats the cycle with his own children. 'You will never amount to anything. You'll never be as good as your sister/brother. I knew you would let us down.' These are all familiar phrases to the children of the accusing father.

Can we pause while you check out if any of the above fit your experience? You can't disown a problem until you first own it. These are some of the common distortions that our experience and our enemy will fling at us concerning the nature of God. Distortions are best identified when they are held in parallel with the real thing. If your image of God is distorted in any of the above ways then I want to present you with a checklist of commonly encountered lies about God, but I would like to parallel them with some truth about God. Apply this checklist to your current view of Him. If you find you can tick any of the lies about God as being your perceptions then I urge you to read, memorise and meditate on (take apart, dissect, chew over, savour – see Chapter 10 for some help on this) the Bible verses which accompany the parallel truth about God. These verses are not just here to pad out the space; they are here to be wilfully applied. They are not proof texts; they're medicine!

LIES ABOUT GOD	TRUTH ABOUT GOD
Distant and uninterested	Intimate and involved. God is passionate about you; you are the apple of His eye (Psa. 17:8; 139:1–18; Isa. 49:15–16).
Uncaring and insensitive	Kind and compassionate. God has a heart that aches and longs to be with you (Psa. 103:8–14; Jer. 31:3; Rom. 2:4; Eph. 2:7).
Stern and demanding	Accepting and overwhelmed with love for you. God is a smiling God (Zeph. 3:17; Rom. 15:7).
Passive and cold	God is warm and affectionate. He is tender and demonstrative towards you (Isa. 40:11; Hos. 11:3–4; 1 John 3:1).
Absent or too busy for you	Always with you and always eager to be with you. He delights in you (Jer. 31:20; Heb. 13:5).

LIES ABOUT GOD	TRUTH ABOUT GOD
Impatient and angry, disappointed and not satisfied with you	God is patient and slow to anger. He approves of you. He likes you as well as loves you, because He wants to, not because He has to (Exod. 34:6; 2 Pet. 3:9).
Mean, cruel and abusive	Loving, gentle and protective of you (Psa. 18:2; Isa. 42:3).
God is trying to take all the fun out of your life	God is trustworthy. He is for you, He wants the very best for you, He wants to give you life to the full (Lam. 3:22–23; John 10:10; Rom. 12:2).
Controlling or manipulative	God is full of grace and mercy. He gives you freedom to fail (Luke 15:11–24; Heb. 4:15–16).
God is condemning or unforgiving towards you	He is continually forgiving and tender-hearted towards you. His arms are always open for you (Psa. 130:3–4; 1 John 1:9).
God is a disapproving perfectionist	God is proud of you as His growing child, you are His workmanship. God is never disillusioned with you for He has no illusions about you and yet is totally committed to you (Eph. 2:10; Heb. 12:5–11).

Remember for every lie that you can tick you have some truth to embrace and some passages to memorise!

MUTUAL LOVE

In 1995, I was involved in a horrendous car crash. I had been doing an evening as part of a series of teaching on evangelism at a church in Stratford and was on my way home, on a dark and rainy night, on the M40. Just between junctions 4 and 3 on a flyover I was overtaken by a car which, in pulling in in front of me, actually clipped my front wing sending me (and him!) into a triple spin at 70 mph! I readily confess that the first word that left my lips was not 'Jesus', I wish it had been! But it *was* the *second*, in the form of a fervent and somewhat urgent prayer! In the course of spinning across the motorway, my car collided with the central reservation, bounced off and then hit a concrete wall on the outside lane head on, leaving the car a complete right-off and still straddling the first lane of the motorway. After some moments of struggling to extricate myself from the car by climbing over the back seat and getting out through the rear door, I was limping my way up the hard shoulder when what was left of my car was hit by a lorry! God was clearly with me and I lived to tell the tale. But it is not an experience I would recommend! The reason I tell you the story is that the next day the most haunting image I had, the one which kept replaying itself in my mind, the one for which I eventually had to get prayer, was not of the crash itself. Rather, it was the scene etched in my memory of me driving away from the house early that morning on my way to my meeting, and of my two children standing at my bedroom window waving me goodbye. The terrible thought that kept going through my mind was that that might have been the last time I saw them or they me. Had God not preserved me (and I have no doubt that it was He who did so) my two children might now be without their father. I can't begin to describe the anguish that I felt about that, like a physical pain ripping at my heart. It's a measure of my love, as daddy, for my kids.

Nor can I adequately describe to you how I still feel (and it must have happened hundreds of times by now) every time I return to my home from a day's work. I know as I put my key in the front door lock that I will have to get through the door quickly and I will have to speedily divest myself of various bags, laptop, mobile. The reason being that within seconds my two children will hurl themselves at me, either down the full length of the hall (and it is a long hall!) or from about the fourth stair up! I would literally have to catch them before they do me or themselves some serious damage in their enthusiasm to express their joy and delight at seeing their daddy again. That is exactly what they will be shouting out, all the way down the stairs or hall, Freddi and Josh both crying out, 'Daddy, Daddy, Daddy, Daddy.' They have always done it, since they could first walk. It's a measure of my kids' love for their daddy. Mutual love.

DADDY

These two experiences are the closest I can come to relating to the biblical story that Jesus described as the best picture of the relationship between God and us. You will find this truth best experienced in Luke 15:11–32 and it is the story of the Prodigal Son. I don't think we can do better than end this chapter by reading through that story which Jesus told, and asking Him for fresh insight and revelation on how its truth can impact our lives.

It is a vivid picture, which realistically highlights the reactions of its four main protagonists. And, like much of the Bible, it makes an even more vivid impact if we understand some of the cultural backdrop against which the story was told.

The first protagonist is the son who chooses to leave home. It was culturally acceptable for a son to gain rights of inheritance and even marriage at the critical turn of age between 12 and 13. At this point a Jewish boy went through the rite of passage known as Bar Mitzvah, which literally means 'son of the promise' and refers to his inheritance under God's covenant as a son both of Abraham and his earthly dad. For the duration of his teens he would now be acknowledged as what the Bible terms a 'youth' (Hebrew word – '*naar*', which literally means a 'doer of heroic deeds for God'). Youths had some of the responsibilities and privileges of adulthood but not all. For example, they were exempt from some temple taxes and from military duties. So, whilst it was legally possible for a son to inherit at an early age, a Jewish family would view it as an extreme insult if he were to ask for his inheritance before the death of his father. To do so would basically be to treat your father as though he were dead. So Jesus' story starts with a gross insult, cast in the face of a loving and providing Dad, as the Son rebelliously determines to go his own way, do his own thing, and have what material provisions he feels he is entitled to.

There then follows a vivid and drawn-from-life portrayal of the second set of protagonists in the story. These are the young man's friends, who turn out to be what my parents would have called 'fair weather friends'! So when the going is good they are with him, and when the going gets bad they go! It is a good portrayal of fickle and superficial relationships based on materialism and selfishness.

As external circumstances now lurch from bad to worse, the son's internal reaction similarly reaches the pits! He ends up not only feeding pigs in a pigsty, but even trying to eat their leftovers. Again it is important culturally to understand what this would mean to a Jew, for whom pigs were unclean animals. Involvement with them would make an individual ritually unclean before God!

Consequently, the son, in his utter desperation, determines to return to his father, not only humbled by his experience, but also crushed by his perception of how his father will view and receive him. He feels that he has lost the right to sonship and that he will deserve his father's disappointment and disapproval. He is convinced that his father will now remain aloof, accusing, abusive and may even potentially absent himself from relationship with his son. Again, culturally, all of these attitudes were possible, and even acceptable out-workings of dis-inheritance.

BUT ...

This brings us to a wonderful description of the third protagonist, the father, in verse 20 of Luke 15. The picture is of a father who is proactively looking out for his lost son. A father whose response is compassionate and intimate. Remember that contact with an unclean Jew made you unclean also, but none of this stops the father throwing his arms around his son and kissing him. A small but telling point for Jesus' audience would have been the description of the father 'running' to his son. For a patriarchal figure in the Jewish family, to run was deemed a matter of great indignity and loss of face. But this dad can't get to his son quickly or intimately enough, he doesn't wait for his son to come to him, but runs out and meets him part way.

The fourth protagonist is the elder brother, but that is a

whole other ball game! You might want to muse on what it is to stay in relationship with the Father but still to work as though *earning* your sonship! I know most of what I have stated above is very self-evident, but it is the kind of biblical picture that can change our own hearts and experience of God as a Daddy. This is the God who celebrates over us, throws a party on our behalf, kills the fatted calf, clothes us with His own robes of righteousness and re-instates us to sonship by putting the family ring on our finger. Small wonder then that God is described in Scripture as a Father who sings, dances, claps and even whistles over us (Isa. 5:26)!

So, where are we then by the end of Chapter 4? We have begun to let God pull out what is on the inside. We have started to grapple with an understanding of our identity and are ruthlessly prepared not to hide behind a projected external image or an internal negative self-image. Now we are up for it; to learn to live and breathe and have our being in God's image, which He is working in us. We are heading for the point where our primary identity is first and foremost who God says we are. And what is this? That:

1. We are a new creation, with all the old definitions gone (2 Cor. 5:17).

2. We are clothed with the gift of righteousness – His not ours! And we are cleansed and forgiven (Rom. 8:12; 2 Cor. 5:21).

3. This is not a whim or a phase, we are now eternal beings and joint heirs with Christ (1 Pet. 1:4; Rev. 3:21).

4. Our safety and security lies in the fact that we have been chosen by God in Christ (1 Pet. 2:9).

5. Our identity is very simple, we have been legally adopted by the best Daddy in the world and have become children of God (John 1:12; Rom. 8:14–17).

If these first four chapters have been of help to you, but you feel that there is still unfinished ground, then you might need to continue to enlighten your mind and soften your heart by further reading as well as by seeking some prayer and ministry from trusted friends. If that is the case let me point you towards some books. They are listed at the end of the chapter. At the very least read the third, sixth and last books and then talk and pray them over with a friend – reflect on what God has said to you through them.

I would like to finish with a quote from Mike Bickle's book, *Passion for Jesus*. If this has been a historic area of struggle for you, why don't you write this out in the most creative way you can and carry it on you round your neck, or in the front of your Bible, or put it over your bedhead, or at eye-level opposite the loo!

My Father is a watching, running, weeping, laughing, embracing, kissing God. He is an encouraging, affirming, praising, affectionate kind of God. He is a God who loves me so much He cannot keep from embracing me. I am the apple of His eye. He is a God who loves my friendship and just wants me to be with him. A God who enjoys my company even in my failure and mistakes, because he sees the sincere intentions of my heart. A God whom I don't have to strive to make happy, because he has always been happy with me from the second I turned to him. He is a Father who is always cheering me on from the sidelines. He enthusiastically calls me His son.

Further Reading

Anderson, Neil, *Living Free in Christ* (Monarch, 1993).

Bickle, Mike, *Passion for Jesus* (Kingsway, 1994).

Lucas, Jeff, *Rediscovering the Father Heart of God* (Crossway, 1997).

McClung, Floyd, *The Father Heart of God* (Kingsway, 1985).

McDonald, Gordon, *Ordering Your Private World* (Highland Books, 1987).

McGee, Robert, *Search for Significance* (Nelson Word, 1998).

Manning, Brennan, *Ragamuffin Gospel* (Scripture Press, 1995).

Pytches, Mary, *Who am I?: Discovering your Identity in Christ*
(Hodder & Stoughton, 1999).

Stibbe, Mark, *From Orphans to Heirs* (BRF, 1999).

Chapter 5

'IT IS FOR FREEDOM ...' (GALATIANS 5:1)

It's funny how life goes in stages. I can remember a few years ago when it seemed as though the whole of our social life revolved around going to friends' weddings. Because I do a lot of public speaking, I found myself getting a lot of invitations to speak at those weddings. And because I am an evangelist we also often found ourselves seated at the reception with groups of the most intransigent unbelievers, presumably in the hope that I would convert them all! But life does go in stages and we are now at the place where we can observe some of our younger friends getting invited to all of their peers' weddings (one such friend had ten wedding invitations in the course of the last year!).

For us, the current stage that we find ourselves in is watching many of our peers, and slightly younger, start a family, with subsequent invitations to speak at a variety of dedications! One of our close friends who stands at five foot nothing in her stockinged feet and who is prone to producing large babies was recently booked in for a Caesarean section for the birth of her second child. Even as I was writing this, another of our friends was within three weeks of the same event and looking and feeling as though she could do with it having happened a month ago! And of course I started the introduction to this book with a story about the birth of our son Joshua.

BORN AGAIN?

All of this serves to remind me that whilst birth is an entirely natural process, it is not always a smooth one. As the baby makes its due bid for freedom and light, it is always possible that the birth may need to be aided. We have some friends whose baby was delivered with the use of forceps (used to grip the baby's head) in the process of delivery! Babies' heads are very soft and only begin to firm up several weeks after birth, so for the first few weeks of this baby's life it had a rather pointed head with red indentation marks on the sides of the skull! I guess the extreme in aided delivery is the Caesarean section, where surgery is needed to cut the baby free and to enable life, growth and maturity. It seems to me that what holds true for being born also holds true for being born again! When Jesus spoke of the necessity of this in the life of any Christian believer (John 3), was it that He was merely indicating the need for a total brand new start, which the New Testament writer Paul picked up in 2 Corinthians 5:17, or was there more behind the analogy which Jesus used? Was He also thinking of the difficulties sometimes encountered in producing new birth? And perhaps of the process of growth, development and maturity that follows on from birth, a theme picked up by New Testament author Peter in 1 Peter 2:2?

Certainly some people become Christians as part of a very natural and easy flowing process, with little evidence of physical, emotional, mental, relational or spiritual trauma. Work done by a man called John Finney for the British and

Foreign Bible Society and printed in 1992 under the title of *Finding Faith Today*, indicates that for most people, finding faith in Christ is a process rather than a crisis. Indeed his survey indicated that 63 per cent of the 500 Christians he surveyed came to faith in Christ over an average four-year process rather than in a 'Damascus Road', crisis conversion.

So, viewing conversion as a journey is probably both more realistic and more natural than viewing it as a sudden incident, although of course that does happen for some. So perhaps the analogy of impregnation, conception and gestation is a good one, when seeds of thought, experience, hope, doubt, conviction of sin and so on, grow in someone's life to the point where they give birth to a desire or a decision to follow the Jesus who can make a difference in these areas. But even though 'process conversion' is prevalent, still for most people being born again isn't a natural and unaided process. For many of us it has involved the need for 'aided' birth and delivery or even for spiritual 'surgery'. It would be a wonderful thing if somewhere in the process of conversion we automatically had all our past hurts, thoughts, fears, anxieties, hopes and dreams completely removed or fulfilled, and that we became then both spiritually free and totally whole! But the reality is that the wholeness or maturity which Paul refers to in Colossians 1:28 is something which has to be worked for.

Whilst our salvation cannot be earned and is totally free (provided for us at the cost of the blood of the Son of God) nonetheless having received it gratefully it is we, in co-operation with God, who then have to 'work out our salvation' (Phil. 2:12). The reality is that if God were to impact us with sufficient Holy Spirit power to change everything in our lives that needed changing all in one go He would probably blow every emotional, spiritual, physical, mental and relational fuse in our entire systems! In addition to that, God is not a Fixer of Problems, but rather a Father of People who is looking more for a meaningful relationship than miraculous readjustments.

ACCESS THE ACCOUNT

So, we have something of a tension emerging. When we become Christians and embark on our journey of following the Way who is Jesus Christ (John 14), we are indeed 'a new creation, the old has gone, the new has come!' (2 Cor. 5:17) and yet our salvation has to be worked out; we have to work hard in co-operation with God and others to present one another whole in Christ. And the reality is that we bring with us on our journey a whole pile of baggage from our pasts. The good news is that this gospel of Jesus Christ is a Gospel of Freedom. ('It is for freedom that Christ has set us free' – Gal. 5:1.) The issue is one of *appropriating* that which God has already done for us in His Son. I have in my time met some extremely wealthy people, who appear to have attained their wealth by never spending a penny and by never being generous in heart or in bank balance! On that simplistic level it doesn't matter what you have in God's heavenly bank account if you don't make use of it, live in the good of it, be generous with it and access the account. I write this chapter on freedom to help us do exactly that.

I propose elsewhere in this book that three keys to spiritual freedom and maturity are knowing God, knowing yourself and knowing the enemy. The Bible exhorts us to be not unaware of the schemes and methods of the enemy (2 Cor. 2:11). Satan is a legalist and will take any legal territory which we give him or which has been handed over to him on our behalf. One of the few occasions in the Bible when Satan is hauled into the very presence of God is in the storyline found in the book of Job. God enquires of Satan as to where he has been and Satan's reply is a telling one. He says (Job 1:7) words to the effect that, 'I have been striding up and down upon the earth/my territory'. The phrase is actually a judicial phrase meaning he has been on his own legal property. When Adam and Eve literally or metaphorically rebelled against God and first sinned, the result was the fall of the whole of created order, and not just of humankind. In effect, this legally delivered over into Satan's hands access to that created order and to humanity, ie you and me!

ENEMY ACCESS!

There are a number of access routes that give the enemy legal territory to come in and influence us. Let's start by looking at our history and at hereditary curses. In effect, curses are the negative or flip side of blessings. They are mentioned over 200 times in the Bible, although God puts a clear emphasis on the positive, as blessings are mentioned over 400 times. Both blessings and curses are words, objects or actions that are charged with supernatural power and their effects can be passed down through the generations. The power of words is well-documented and understood in the Bible and you might want to check out some of the following passages to help your understanding of this. Have a look at Genesis 27:27–40; Proverbs 11:9; 12:18 and 8:21.

Some actions and objects can evoke either a blessing or a curse and this is explored in Scripture, in Exodus 20:4–5 and 1 Samuel 16:13. Deuteronomy 28 provides a key passage wholly devoted to both blessings and curses and to their cause and effect. Basically, blessing comes from listening to God and obeying what He says, and curses come from *not* listening to God and deliberately *not* doing what He says. One of the wonderful aspects about becoming a Christian is that we are no longer simply victims of our past or of the past behaviour of people influential in our lives. According to Proverbs 26:2, curses can only take a hold if there is a legitimate cause or, if you like, a 'landing strip' for the enemy to coast into our life. However, where there *is* legitimate cause, words will often find an entrance into our lives and begin to take effect. When that is the case, repeated cycles or patterns where the same things often or always seem to go wrong, can provide a clue as to when a curse is operating.

Some years ago I was involved in pastoring a Christian band and had first-hand opportunity of observing generational curses at work in the life of one of the band members. I don't think before or since I have seen such a strong pattern of accidents, negative circumstances, financial and personal misfortune, consistently and repeatedly outworked over a number of years. Exploration indicated that there was indeed a generational curse not dealt with, unrecognised and stretching back at least two generations.

Certainly experience has indicated the reality of hereditary curses. When seeking to move from Bognor Regis to church plant into Portsmouth we attempted for two years to sell our maisonette and, for no apparently good reason, were unable to do so. This was immensely frustrating, as for the first year of the birth of the Portsmouth church we were literally commuting backwards and forwards, a 50-mile round trip, at least three times a week, and we felt very isolated and cut off from our support base and from the geographical territory that God had called us to. It was only when a friend of ours with a marked discernment and deliverance ministry came and prayed around our maisonette (which had previously been owned by active spiritualists) and prayed off us a 'curse of poverty' that the maisonette then immediately shifted and we found the right place in Portsmouth! Once since then we have had a similar poverty curse prayed off us. This time the repeated pattern was different. Although we had sufficient funds coming in (we live by the gospel and the faithfulness of God), they would immediately drain away because of unforeseen and unexpected household bills. These included major mistakes made by our mortgage company and the Inland Revenue! Again, when a curse of poverty was addressed, we felt this cycle break, and have lived in the good of that ever since.

SIGNS AND SYMPTOMS

We recently had a family medical dictionary delivered to our door from a book club. My wife had been wanting one for some while and I must admit that it was with a certain vicarious glee that I started to thumb through the pages. Have you ever done this? I started off reading the book feeling perfectly fine. By the time I had finished, I was utterly convinced that I had got every symptom of every disease under the sun and a few that had probably not yet been invented! When we are looking for signs and symptoms of hereditary curses, it is important that we don't go on any kind of historical or psychological dig! That's why what follows is littered with 'may' or 'can'. Equally, it is important that we don't 'throw the baby out with the bath water' and that we *do* wise up to some of the signs and symptoms of the strategy of the enemy in our life. What is needed is discernment, wisdom and fellowship in all these matters.

HEALTH TARGETS

So, with that little warning note in place, a quick look at Deuteronomy 28:20,28,34,65 will indicate that mental or emotional breakdown *may* be a sign and a symptom of a generational curse. Mental torment, a perpetual unease, extreme negativity or despair *could* all be symptomatic. Key words here to watch out for *could* be 'confusion' and 'depression'.

Similarly, a repeated cycle of debilitating illness or chronic sickness, indicating a destructive force at work behind the scenes is alluded to in Deuteronomy 28:21–22,27–28,35,59,61. Key words to watch out for here *could* be 'incurable', 'fearful', 'prolonged' and 'lingering'.

Deuteronomy 28:18 indicates that where there is infertility, impotence, barrenness, miscarriage and other related problems (affecting a large number of people in the Western hemisphere now) that there *may* be a generational curse to be dealt with. Certainly our experience as a couple has been a three-stage process of God breaking curses from our lives when it came to our desire and ability to have children. We had been told medically that we would not be able to have children. Then God stepped in both prophetically and with healing. His healing came in three stages, on three specific occasions when we were prayed for and with. I would call the first a kind of 'emotional healing' when I was prayed for concerning past sexual sins and self-image issues. The second I would say effected 'physical healing' and the third, some three months later, involved the breaking off of generational curses through Nikki's side of the family connected to Free Masonry (Free Masonry often produces a sense of darkness and secrecy and involves overt curses in connection with death, and often aimed against women).

FAMILY TARGETS

Because God is the first team and the first family (Father, Son and Holy Spirit) and because the enemy hates God, so too, the enemy hates team and family. Deuteronomy 28:41 shows how the breakdown of marriage and family alienation *can* be the direct result of a generational curse. A past family history of separation and divorce *can* be a further symptom, as too can children taken captive by the enemy, eg through involvement in drugs, rebellion and so on. A history of suicides or unnatural, untimely deaths *may*, again, be an indication of a curse being outworked.

FINANCIAL TARGETS

In Deuteronomy 28:17,29,47–48, debt and poverty *can* be a hallmark of a curse. The symptom is often not so much obvious poverty as a constant sense of struggling with finances, of being in debt, even where there is enough income to the household or family. This is the kind of curse that I alluded to earlier, of which we've had firsthand experience.

ACCIDENT PRONE?

Freak accidents, things always going wrong and circumstances turning our badly (remember my Christian band leader?) *might* indicate a generational curse (Deut. 28:29).

CAUSES AND SOURCES

If you have already looked at Deuteronomy 28 (chapter 27 is worth a glance as well) and care to look further, into Genesis

12:3 and Jeremiah 17:5–8, then you will find that God Himself can be the cause of a curse. This is primarily because God is a God of love, eager and active always to be a source of blessing, but love demands choice (to love or not to love) and choice demands consequence (ie blessing or cursing). To reject God can be to embrace a curse.

And if reaction against God can be the cause of a curse so too can people rightly representing God. Examples of this can be found in Joshua 6:26, 2 Samuel 1:21, 1 Kings 16:34 and Matthew 11:24. Do look at at least a couple of these references so that you can see that I am not making this stuff up!

Alternatively, curses can find their source in Satan, who is keen always to curse, never to bless. Even 'apparent' blessings (for example 'healings' from New Age healers or spiritualist churches) always come at a cost. The sting in the tail is often fear or anxiety for the one 'healed'. Ungodly covenants/ promises/partnerships can be the source of a satanic curse. Check out Exodus 23:32 and 2 Corinthians 6:14. Perhaps, as you would expect, people who are representing Satan can also curse others. An example is seen in Numbers 22:6.

And, finally, what of a self-imposed curse? I have on a number of occasions had to deal with people prone to depression and/or sickness who have effectively cursed themselves at an earlier time by strongly, deliberately and act- ively 'wishing themselves dead' or deliberately and realistically contemplating suicide. The effect of this is as a self-imposed curse. An example can be found in Genesis 27:11–13.

'I WANT TO BREAK FREE ...'

Just as birth is a process, so too is attaining freedom. But be encouraged; once a curse is broken it is broken down the family line. Ultimately the only effective and permanent way of breaking any curse is through Christ. His name is above every other name including any generational curse and is more powerful than any curse that ever has or ever can affect us (Phil. 2:10–11). Freedom from generational curses starts when:

1. As God's kids we recognise that His desire and ability to bless far outweighs any incidents of cursing.

2. Our freedom grows as we grab hold of/recognise/ meditate on/eat and drink the truth that on the cross of Jesus Christ a vital exchange took place. *He* actually became cursed so that *we* might receive blessing. It was not just that He became sin so that we might become forgiven or even that He became bruised in order that we might be healed. It is *all* of these things. Have a good look at Galatians 3:13–14 and 1 John 3:8.

3. We take a measure of personal responsibility and accept our part in the cause or effect of any such curse. This will often lead us to repentance and renunciation; an active wilful rejection of everything involved in such a curse. On occasions, that may actually mean getting rid of unhelpful physical objects and reminders linked to that curse, or to those people. On the DNA discipleship training course, which I am involved in leading, it is not infrequent for God to speak through a word of knowledge into the lives of our trainees, and for them to respond by physically 'binning' personal items that tie them to a curse in their history. We have seen quite valuable items such as wallets, rings, necklaces, mobile phones, thrown into a bin at the front of a meeting during a response time, as a symbolic but deeply meaningful expression of the desire to break free. Equally, we have seen a number of sentimental items with emotion-

al attachments go the same way (photographs, letters …).
On these occasions the subsequent testimony has been of
remarkable freedom gained (Rev. 12:11). Sometimes the
objects binned represent past sin (a sin bin!) but on other
occasions they represent a simple desire to symbolically
remove all links with past generational curses.

4. We actively receive forgiveness, and deliberately forgive
   others. This is a *choice* that you make with God's help. You
   choose both to give and to receive forgiveness. It is *not*
   primarily a feeling that you wait for. Rather, it is an act of
   godly will, and for those of you reading this book who feel
   that your will power is weak or damaged, we'll be looking
   at that in the next chapter as the exercise of your will is an
   important aspect of walking in freedom with Jesus.

5. We involve other godly women and men, who can pray
   for us, care for us and lay hands on us with faith-filled
   prayer. This is not a 'go it alone' process.

6. There's an expectation that things will change and be
   different. This is important, as it is on hope that faith is
   built. Keeping some kind of record, reflection process, a
   spiritual journal or prayer diary, will help you recognise
   the answers to prayer that God is giving.

7. Finally, we give thanks and praise to God for the work He
   has accomplished. This should not, however, be done as
   some form of wishful thinking, but rather as a direct
   response to the changes that you have seen and felt God
   make in your life. Praise and worship consistently alters our
   perspective and often puts a seal on the work of God in our
   lives. As my mum would say, 'Don't forget your Ps & Qs!'

MIND AND IMAGINATION

Many Christians struggle to believe that they can be free in the area of their mind and imagination, and on a daily basis, battle with the appropriateness or inappropriateness of their 'thought life'. Writing (as I must!) as a man, it is all too easy to hone this down into the arena of sexual thoughts and fantasies. For a male, that which is seen is often the stimulus for that which is then dwelt upon mentally and/or fantasised over. My attempts to work with and understand females better causes me to think that the arena is no less marked for them, although often perhaps it is more a matter of emotions stimulating their mind and imaginations sexually: things felt more than seen. However, although this is an important facet of the mind and imagination, it is only one facet. There are many other arenas to which the mind and imagination can find themselves drawn away from God, and therefore become focused more into bondage than into freedom. For example ...

- How is your thought life concerning your self-worth and self-image (see Chapters 1–3)?
- How do your mind and imagination cope with comparison of others and of their possessions?
- How do your mind and imagination cope when it comes to other appetites, like food, alcohol or physical exercise?

Just why is it such an important area?

BATTLE FOR THE MIND

It is important, because the mind is under daily bombardment, and all too often in a fallen world can feel like something of a battle zone. The Bible is clear on this with a variety of very practical warnings. 'Do not eat the bread of a selfish man, or desire his delicacies; for as he thinks within himself, so he is. He says to you, "Eat and drink!" but his heart is not with you'

(Prov. 23:6–7, NASB). This daily battleground and its consequences are made clear in Romans 8:5, NRSV: 'For those who live according to the flesh set their minds on the things of the flesh, but those who live according to the Spirit set their minds on the things of the Spirit.'

THE MIND AND REVELATION

God's revelation concerning His love and His plans and desires for us and for our destiny, primarily impacts us in our hearts. But the appropriation of God's revelation has to move from our hearts to our heads and our wills if we are to outwork it. Without *heartfelt* revelation, the people of God lose their way and throw off restraint and ultimately perish (Prov. 29:18), but it is equally true that without appropriation of that revelation and a *head* understanding, the people of God also perish (Hos. 4:6).

THE MIND AND IDENTITY

If it is true that God is more interested in who we are than in what we do, and in how we do what we do than in what we do (see Chapters 1–3 again), then the importance of a free mind and imagination becomes obvious. It is in our mind and imagination that the most impact is made on who we think we are as well as on what we do. Every feeling you ever had about yourself (or anything else for that matter) was preceded by a thought. Only grow to understand that, and a significant key to freedom is yours.

THE MIND SUBMITTED

When you become a Christian you do not kiss your brains

goodbye! Indeed in very many ways your mind comes alive and alight by the revelation of God. I have even seen God step in and supernaturally heal dyslexics who couldn't read His Word before. A friend of mine in my days in the East End was a builder who couldn't and wouldn't read a word, but on conversion to Christ, was instantaneously enabled to read, study and understand the Bible.

So, although becoming a Christian is not a 'leap in the dark', rather more a 'step into the light', nonetheless the mind has to *learn* to submit to the Holy Spirit. Our minds like to think that they are in charge, but actually we weren't designed to live like that. Before you were a Christian you were spiritually dead to Christ, dead in sin and a captive to the law of sin and death (Rom. 6:19–23; 8:2). Under those circumstances your mind dominated your existence with its own desire and will. And probably in equal measure your body dominated with its own drives and instincts. But when you became a Christian you became alive in spirit and subject to the law of life and of the Holy Spirit. A new line of authority was established in your existence. Under this new line of authority, the Holy Spirit communicates directly with your spirit, which informs your mind, which in turn informs your body. There's been a change in the chain of command! In this way we are no longer slaves to our appetites, be they bodily or mental/emotional. This is another reason why the area of freedom in our mind and imagination is so important.

THE MIND AND CHOICES

As a friend of mine, Gerald Coates, is fond of saying, 'If you will but choose right you will come out right.' The gospel of Jesus Christ is a gospel of freedom. Freedom to choose, freedom to serve, freedom to submit – choices are made in the arena of the will. Our will (that which determines, chooses and decides) works in co-operation with our mind. So self-activation, the mind and the imagination are all interconnected and vitally important. In the next chapter we will look more closely at the freedom that comes with a restored will, and at bondage that comes from an impaired will.

SOME DEFINITIONS

The Bible appears to be ambivalent about how it describes the make-up of humanity. There are those who see in the Bible a definition of humanity as 'tri-partite', or made up of three 'parts' comprising spirit, soul (including mind, which is usually translated as 'heart' in the Bible) and body. However, these phrases are sometimes used interchangeably in the Bible and even sometimes to mean something completely different. (The 'soul' can also sometimes be translated as 'corpse'!) Although there is some usefulness in thinking about the different emphases represented by these three different areas, it is probably more important to remember that the Hebrew worldview saw the whole of life and existence as spiritual and involving God. The gospel is a holistic message about God in all of His fullness to every part of us. So human beings don't either in reality or biblically divide neatly into three parts, but are rather a fusion of body, soul and spirit, mind, will and imagination, physical and spiritual.

But it is probably helpful when we come to think about the mind and imagination to have some clarity of definition. When I use the word 'mind' I am talking primarily about our thoughts, our desires, our inclinations and purposes, our intentions, our way of thinking, our memory, our opinion and our direction. When I speak about 'imagination' I am thinking primarily of the power to form a mental image of something, which is not actually present. Incidentally, when mentioning the word 'fantasy' I am describing there the free play of creative imagination. Unfortunately the word, particularly for the Christian, has come to denote something negative. I would like to suggest that fantasy is not in and of itself inherently wrong. Fantasy is clearly a function of the imagination, and imagination is clearly to be kept on a tight rein, for the mind can be a breeding ground for sin. But it is worth remembering that God is the ultimate imaginative Creator. He fantasised and conceived us and our world in His mind before we ever existed (Psa. 139). God Himself thinks, desires, remembers ... He is clearly described as having a personality, which includes a mind and an imagination. Indeed, He is described in several places in the Old Testament (Gen. 6:6–7; 18:20–33) as changing His mind. We have mind, imagination and fantasy because God has, and He made us in His image!

So it really is time to take a stand and fight for what God has given us and, where necessary, to take issue with our minds and imaginations so that they get into line! The renewing of our minds is a process and not a one-stop conversion experience (Rom. 12:1–2). And it is certainly not a process that happens magically without our engagement. If life and peace, wholesome imagination and creativity are all taken from you, if you find yourself mentally lazy or emotionally apathetic and weary, then I would urge you to engage, to be angry at the thief who comes to steal, and to pick up your weapons and fight for your inheritance.

AS A PERSON THINKS SO HE IS ...

The battle is on for our mind. Perhaps that is why part of the full, close-quarters combat armour of God (the '*panoplia*' talked about in Ephesians 6) includes a helmet of salvation for the guarding of our minds. Many of our thoughts are not God-centred, so it is important to recognise where they come from, as knowing our weaknesses can help us fight them. According to the Bible 'thoughts' come …

- from God
- from the 'world' – all that comes at us from the outside.
- from the 'flesh' – which is biblical shorthand for the internal life of sin, which so easily tangles us up.
- from the 'devil' and the demonic realm as evidenced in 2 Corinthians 11:3.
- from the past – the enemy reminds us of our past to rob us of our future. God reminds us of our past to release us into our future.

Biblically, most spiritual strongholds are to be found in the arena of our mind, and need to be dealt with there, before they are ever dealt with in the lives of other people or in territorial spirits or in demonic presences.

So, how about a kind of 'do-it-yourself' checklist concerning ungodly mindsets? I'm determined to be as relevant and practical as possible. It may be that you can helpfully identify one or more of these tendencies in your own thinking, remembering again that we need to own a problem preparatory to disowning it.

INDEPENDENT THINKING

This is to allow, develop and maintain a mentality which does not take God, His existence, His plans or His purposes into account. The warning in Titus 1:15, is clear: 'To the pure, all things are pure, but to those who are corrupted and do not believe, nothing is pure. In fact, both their minds and consciences are corrupted.'

ANXIOUS THINKING

The spirit of the age is 'angst'. The pace of change, pressure of life, pursuit of materialism, and information overload are all potential tools in the hands of the 'thief of peace'. Anxiety, worry and fear, with their symptoms of insomnia, tension and stress and the outlets of impatience, irritability, road rage and the like, indicate the prevalence of anxious thinking. Philippians 4:4–6 encourages us to 'in everything, by prayer and petition, with thanksgiving, present your requests to God. And the peace of God, which transcends all understanding, will guard your hearts and your minds in Christ Jesus'.

WANDERING THINKING

Contrary to common perceptions, a mind not fixed God-ward does not simply empty itself or stay in neutral! Nature and your mind abhor a vacuum! So a mind not fixed on God will be a distracted and a wandering mind, and one prone to being filled by the enemy. A good example of this can be seen in the life of David and his illicit affair with Bathsheba (found in 2 Sam. 11 and 12).

PROUD THINKING

Pride and rebellion are root sin issues stretching right back to Satan's own fall from God. Proud thinking is a dangerous mindset; 'Jesus turned and said to Peter, "Get behind me, Satan! You are a stumbling-block to me; you do not have in mind the things of God, but the things of men" ' (Matt. 16:23).

INTELLECTUAL THINKING

Reliance on self or the finite capacity of the human brain to solve the human heart and condition, is a hallmark of intellectual thinking. As a Christian, your mind is a gift from God, but the warning is clear; do not be led astray by the brightest human minds 'For the Kingdom of God is not a matter of words but of power' (1 Cor. 4:20, GNB); alternatively 'we have the mind of Christ' (1 Cor. 2:16). This is never to be an excuse for under-using the mental gifts God has given us, nor for avoiding understanding. But recognition of our limitations and acknowledgement of our motivations are vital. Never read anything in order to appear wise. Knowing answers to difficult questions will not help you nearly as much as spiritual discipline. Even after profound scholarship you still need to know God, for He is the beginning of everything and the teacher of all people (Psa. 94:10).

DISAPPOINTED THINKING

The very word disappointment gives us a clue to its meaning and origin. It literally means an arrangement made for 'an important appointment, which has been missed', and it carries with it a sense of opportunity lost, destiny frustrated, hopes dashed and future thwarted. This is a very debilitating mindset and in my experience it is hard for God to be able to use a Christian with a consistently disillusioned or disappointed mindset. In 2 Samuel 6:8–8:12 you'll see a good example of how the people of God got into the cycle of disappointed thinking and its consequences.

SMALL THINKING

The whole of Psalm 139 is written as an attempt to shift small thinking and to encourage the reader to begin to grapple with the hugeness and goodness of God and His dealings with us. I can do no better than urge you to read it! It is one of the reasons why Nikki and I had it read out at our wedding.

Now, can you identify with any of the above? And if identifying and owning a wrong mindset is half the battle, where do we go from here?

DEFYING STRONGHOLDS, CHANGING MINDSETS

Argentinian revivalist Ed Silvoso defines a spiritual stronghold as 'a mindset impregnated with hopelessness, which accepts as unchangeable something which is contrary to the will of God'. And yet God is true (Num. 23:19) and His promises to us are dependable. He does not mock His people by holding up an impossible picture of unattainable freedom, forever beyond our grasp (John 8:31–32). So strongholds *can* be defied; mindsets *can* be changed. But in my experience this does not come easy or cheap! We know that changing any ingrained habit pattern (eg giving up smoking, cutting down on alcohol, taking up exercise, going on a diet) is really quite difficult. We would be foolish then to imagine that it's going to be easy to bring change to our minds, a key area of spiritual battleground as well as the breeding ground of habit. I have a slow metabolism and a lifestyle which doesn't make consistent dieting easy, so for years, on and off, I fought a weight problem, and I still do. Why on earth would I try to diet for a while and then give up because it is not working? Why should I surrender at my first failure? Why should I call myself a failure at dieting when all too often I will set unrealistic expectations, which then do not materialise because they never could (ie I will lose 7 kg in a month!). Rather, in the defying of strongholds and the changing of mindsets, persistence and realism need to go hand in hand. There is a strength to be found in weakness, in vulnerability, in self-disclosure. Integrity and freedom are not confined to the realms of platonic idealism, where we get it all right at once; but are also to be found in the midst of failure and God-centred choices. None of us have it 'all together'; welcome to Planet Earth! Providing you are prepared to bear that in mind, the following principles should be helpful to you as they have been to me, in learning little by little to take and hold new ground.

LITTLE BY LITTLE ...

How do we see freedom slowly begin to come in the areas of our mind and imagination?

- Firstly, by recognising that freedom is a process, a journey not a destination. Each part of the route needs outworking and exploring with a whole new set of right choices being made in the light of what has happened. This requires patience, courage and wilfulness not to fall into the trap of comparison with the past or with other people. It also requires us to be realistic – we may still lose some battles along the way, but we will win the overall victory. There is no room to fall into the trap of 'I messed up, so I will give up'. Every day is a new day crammed full of God's grace and mercy all over again (Lam. 3:22–23).

- Secondly, our minds and imaginations need to be focused on truth instead of lies. Reading relevant bits of the Bible, writing out truth, sticking God's statements on 'Post-its®' round walls, memorising Scripture; all are essential (Matt. 4:1–11)! What God has said to us we need to say to ourselves. Gradually you'll find that processing truth runs something like this:

    Learning right thinking helps us to
    choose right behaviour which helps us to
    experience right feelings.

- Thirdly, let's understand how vital those around you are. One of the strongest defences you have is your network of relationships. The more isolated you become as a straggler in the army of Jesus Christ the easier it is for you to get picked off by enemy fire from snipers! But these relationships need commitment, honesty, openness, vulnerability, time, depth and fun! They can help us put new boundaries and safeguards in place in our thinking and our imaginations, and hold us accountable to them. Our friends can also witness the change in us and when change and truth fade from our memory remind us of these truths; and in the midst of battles lost or won, have a laugh with us and help us keep our perspective.

- Finally, with increasing freedom comes new attitudes. We begin to realise that we *can* take responsibility for our own life and actions, and for our own thoughts and imaginations. We are *not* the victims of our past any longer. Under the hand of God, we are in control of our lives, and circumstances are not! We can therefore be active in pursuing life's goals and have no need, time or desire to drift or to settle. Rather, we can keep fighting for our inheritance in God (Deut. 30:19–20). This *active* rather than passive attitude also promotes an attitude of thankfulness and gratitude to God. No longer need we blame God or other people – they are not the enemy. The enemy is the enemy! As Christians we have never been guaranteed an easy life, but we have been guaranteed one that is fulfilling and one where God will always be with us (Heb. 13:5–6). Struggle and pain can then be embraced and dealt with, not avoided or denied, as through it there is often a maturing process (1 Pet. 1:7). In all of this our attitude can be one of hopefulness, that things can and will be different (Jer. 29:11). Although our enemy would dearly like to intimidate us in the arenas of our mind and imagination, with our confidence fixed in God, what can he do to us (James 4:7; 1 John 4:4)? And there's more …!

Chapter 6

'... THAT CHRIST HAS SET US FREE' (GALATIANS 5:1)

The freedom that we have in Christ is not automatic. It would be wonderful if it were, but the reality is it is not. Like everything else in the Christian life freedom has to be appropriated actively, it is not simply received passively.

One of my earliest childhood heroes was Houdini. It was through reading about him that I embarked on my own hobby of escapology, which for many years I used as an illustration of the good news of Jesus Christ and the freedom that He brings. Houdini claimed to be able to get out of anything that he was fastened into, and demonstrated this by escaping from police regulation handcuffs, chains, manacles, ankle irons, boxes, crates, straitjackets and prisons, the world over. A story is told that, following a rigorous strip search and incarceration into police cells, Houdini began to work himself free. He first escaped from the chains, manacles, leg irons and padlocks that were fastened around him and then turned his attention to the cell door. It was of a standard, if formidable, design and the lock should have succumbed to his expert manipulations; however, try as he might Houdini was unable to pick the lock. The headlines loomed large in his mind and his imagination: 'Houdini Fails! Escapologist Held Captive!'

Finally, in utter frustration and defeat, Houdini leaned his head wearily against the cell door, only to be precipitated, much to his surprise, into the corridor beyond as the cell door clanged open! The reason why Houdini had been unable to pick the lock open was that it was already open! The gaoler had forgotten to lock it.

Could this story provide a picture of you and me as new Christians? Jesus has unlocked the prison door, but we have to understand that the lock is undone, push the door open and choose to walk free. The freedom which Christ brings us is ultimately freedom from sin (its power and its effects), from suffering (its emotional and relational trauma), from sickness (mental and physical illness) and from Satan (his power, authority and his minions!). But we have to choose life and choose good if we want to see the blessing of God (Deut. 30:15–20).

If it is indeed true that Christian maturity is based on the three pillars of knowing God, knowing ourselves and knowing our enemy, then we must give some attention to this latter. There *is* an enemy, real and personal. Ultimately, evil is never impersonal; it has personality. Three of the main hallmarks of personality (knowledge, will and emotion) are also hallmarks of the demonic. Demons, like their satanic master, possess knowledge (Mark 1:24; Acts 19:15), they have wills (Luke 8:31–33) and they have emotions (James 2:19). A demon, therefore, is not a habit, a mental state or a psychological condition, but a spiritual entity, a part of the kingdom of Satan and subject to that kingdom's hierarchy of fear. These demonic entities can reason and although restless, have personality and intelligence (Matt. 12:43–45). They can enslave and influence people towards evil (Acts 16:16–18). They beg and plead (Mark 5:12) and they rule in the spiritual realm (Eph. 6:12). Both Old and New Testaments indicate that demonic manifestation occurs at different levels in the lives of people. Phrases used to describe the interaction between demons and people include: 'holding captive, tormenting, oppressing, sorely oppressing, afflicting and possessing'. This latter, 'possessing', is a rather disturbing and not wholly accurate translation of a New Testament verb, which would be better rendered 'demonised'. The idea of demonic possession can conjure up unhelpful pictures more reminiscent of the alien creature bursting out of the middle of John Hurt's chest in the film *Alien* than the New Testament! Some have debated about whether a Christian can have a demon, arguing that this is impossible if the Christian's body is indeed the temple of the Holy Spirit. Still others have inverted this argument and asked the question whether a demon may have a Christian! The reality is that Old and New Testaments make allowances for people's personality and for psychological disorders, whilst at the same time affirming the existence of another sphere – that of demonic influence. In my personal and observed experience it is unusual for a Christian not to have *some* measure of need for deliverance from direct enemy activity. Satan and his minions are legalists, and if given any legal territory they will endeavour to inhabit it. To change the analogy, if you lay down a landing strip in lifestyle, then Satan and his minions are likely to seek to land on it!

Points of access can include involvement in the occult or Eastern mysticism, drug abuse, generational curses (see Chapter 5), illicit sex (see Chapter 8), abandoned and un-controlled thought-life, unbridled (even though legitimate) appetites and so on. (Have a look at Chapter 10.) And sin frequently indulged in has the potential for forming a habit, or habitual sin. It is estimated that on average it takes three weeks to make a habit and six weeks to break a habit. Clearly it is a fact of life that we can all have habits (good or bad), of which we are in control. Up to this point we can deal with a sinful habit through confession, repentance, some helpful friendship and accountability (pastoral support). However, if we indulge wilfully and repeatedly in the habit, it is a little like trampling over the same ground again and again. Eventually the ground becomes hard and smooth, and provides a landing strip for enemy activity. Once this has happened, demonic influence can be established and we are then beyond habit and into the realms of captivity. Once this is the case there is *still* a need for confession and repentance, for friendship and accountability (pastoral support), but there will *also* be a need to seek prayer and faith-filled laying on of hands for freedom and deliverance to come in the name of Jesus. This is not something you can or should seek to do on your own. It is a good example of our interdependence upon one another, and of our need to surround ourselves with people who are wiser and more mature than we are in Christ, whose lives are clean in the areas where we are seeking help, and who know the authority they have in the name of Jesus. If you don't know such people already, then find them.

But deliverance is no kind of 'quick fix'. It *may* involve the dramatic removal of a demonic root in our lives; but ultimately it is a process of being changed 'from glory into glory' (2 Cor. 3:18). New Testament salvation is written of in three tenses: 'We have been saved, we are being saved, we will be saved.' So, too, deliverance is spoken of in all three tenses in 2 Corinthians 1:10, 'He has [past] delivered us from such a deadly peril, and he will [future] deliver us. On him we have set our hope that he will continue [present] to deliver us.' All deliverance is found, as is all salvation, and all freedom, in the name of Jesus Christ, who is 'the same yesterday [past], today [present] and for ever [future]' (Heb. 13:8). So actually deliverance + discipline = freedom. And whilst it is certainly true that there is no name that is higher than the name of Jesus Christ (Phil. 2:9), so sometimes in the exercising of self-discipline the word 'NO' to a wrong/bad choice can be just as effective!

Let's look at a crucial area all too rarely taught on in much of the Church. If deliverance + discipline = freedom, some of that discipline involves the godly exercising of our will. That's what this whole next section is about.

WHERE THERE'S A WILL ...!

When God made people He made them in His image, which means that we are not only spiritual, but also emotional, physical, rational and volitional beings. That is to say, we have feelings, bodies, thoughts and a will. My wife, Nikki, and I had cause to go to our solicitor shortly after we were married to draw up our own wills. We discovered the truth in the maxim 'Where there's a will there's a relative!' But the most important kind of will is the freedom and ability Jesus came to restore to us, to choose to do right, and not to do wrong. God is interested in saving the *whole* person (remember, the Greek word for salvation is '*soteria*', meaning wholeness and healing) and not just the spiritual side of us, or the emotional and physical side of us, and so on. God is therefore committed, amongst other things, to restoring our will to us.

The simple truth is that every command God gives, throughout Scripture and in your personal relationship with

Him, is a command directed, before anything else, towards your will. In other words, what will you choose to do in response to God's command? Your will is therefore the bridge between your belief and your action. For the Jew, there was no gap between what he *really* believed and what he *actually* did. If a Jew didn't do it, he didn't believe it! And that's why American Christian author, Jim Wallis, could rightly say, 'What you do on Monday morning is what you really believe; everything else is religion.' Right feelings come from right action, which comes from right choices, which come from right belief (thinking), and *not* the other way round. Too many of us live life in reverse too much of the time, as though life is based on feelings. So, if we feel OK, we'll do OK, which means on a good day with the wind in the right direction, we'll maybe make right choices, if we're lucky, based on right belief! This isn't right, and often won't work.

OUT OF ORDER?

Your Christian journey is like a train. The engine pulling the train is FACT. That is to say, it is a *fact* that there is a God. It is a *fact* that He loves you. It is a *fact* that Jesus Christ is His Son. It is a *fact* that He lived, died and rose from the dead for you. It is a *fact* that as a Christian you are now a child of God.

Following close behind this engine of FACT is FAITH. This is rather like the fuel tender in an old steam train. It's got all the fuel that you need to feed into the facts of your Christian journey. And so you invest your faith in the facts of Christianity. Christianity is not about blind faith, it is not a leap into the dark, but a walk into the light!

Trundling along behind the engine of FACT and the tender of FAITH come the carriages of FEELINGS. I have already said that in salvation, God is interested in the whole of your life, and He wants to save/redeem/buy back your feelings as well. So don't follow traditional evangelical teaching that tells you to ignore your feelings completely, because God wants to spruce them up for you! Which means that when your feelings are on track and all is going smoothly and you are enjoying God and friends around you, you should enjoy your feelings. And when things are *not* going smoothly and your feelings have jumped off the rail (perhaps you're not feeling well, or perhaps it's pre-menstrual tension, or perhaps it's just the weather!) then the answer is – don't live off them. So, when your feelings are good, enjoy them. When your feelings are bad, stuff your feelings! Push through despite them.

I know that sounds simple, but it is really essential to learn how to exercise our will in choosing right and not wrong. So many people have said to me, 'How can I deny my feelings in this area?' The answer is, of course, not to deny your feelings; but neither is it to wallow in them. You don't find Jesus ignoring His feelings in the Garden of Gethsemane in Matthew 26:36–39 (a passage worth looking at), nor do you find Him living off His feelings, for His choice was to do the Father's will.

We would do well to follow Jesus' example when we're assailed by negative feelings: to spend time with God and seek the support of our Christian friends. It isn't spiritual to deny our feelings; Jesus wasn't cut off from God when He admitted how He felt in that garden – indeed, in one sense, He was closer to God than ever, as He admitted to His feelings, yet still committed Himself to obey God's will.

FREE, BUT IMPAIRED?

So, we need to understand that God *won't* violate your will, and Satan *can't*. You have free-will because God Himself has free-will and even, on occasions in the Bible, changes His mind. Have a look at Genesis 6:6–7 and 18:20–33.

You might argue that if Satan can't override our will, how can we get into addiction? The answer is that although Satan can't override our will, he can impair or damage it. Jesus' will was in submission to His Father (John 6:38) and that is our goal too. But Satan will try to impair our will in the following ways.

A WILL DENTED BY SIN

This is Satan's attempt to convince you that the old cycle of 'temptation *must* lead to sin, which *must* lead to habit, which *must* lead to addiction' still stands. The truth of the matter, of course, is that there's no longer a 'must' about it! Before you were a Christian, you were a victim to the law of sin and death, and temptation would automatically lead you into sin. There would be occasional exceptions to this, but the norm for you was sin. When you became a Christian, however, you came out from under the law of sin and death and into the law of grace and the life of the Holy Spirit. The question now is not *when* you sin, but *if* you sin. It is now not the norm for you to sin every time you are tempted. In fact, for you, sin now has to be a conscious choice, and you will be aware as a Christian of grieving the Holy Spirit within you when you make that wrong choice. You and I must learn to deal with temptation, so that it need not lead us into sin, and so that our wills won't be impaired. Because, if we let temptation constantly lead to sin, and if we keep on sinning, then our will gets weaker, and we're heading towards addiction. So the first step to avoid a will impaired by sin is to *reckon* yourself dead to sin (Rom. 6:11).

The next step is to *resist* the devil by first of all submitting yourself to God, rather than trying to fight Satan; you will then find that Satan will have to flee from you (James 4:7).

Thirdly, you must *replace* bad thoughts with good (Phil. 4:8), always remembering that temptation in itself is not sin, for Jesus was tempted in every way as we are, and yet was without sin (Heb. 4:15). Remember, too, that you will never be tempted beyond what you can cope with, for God would not allow that (1 Cor. 10:13), and that the wisest course of action when faced with temptation is described in 2 Timothy 2:22 – run away from it! Don't flirt with temptation, or put yourself in the way of it, because that isn't temptation, it is sin.

Of course, if you're already some way down the addiction road, you'll have found your will weakened because of repeated sin, and you must understand that the remedy for sin is repentance. It may sound simple, but 1 John 1:9 makes it quite clear that if we confess our sins, God does two things: He forgives us and He cleanses us. But we must be clear about this; the Holy Spirit is given to us to make us feel bad when we *are* bad (John 16:8). So there's no point constantly denying the problem; we need to own the problem in order to reject it. And we must be prepared to embrace the ongoing process of getting rid of sin in our lives, rather than always looking for the quick and easy solution.

When there is sin in our life, which has impaired our will, remember that the blood of Jesus Christ will cover what we will first *un*cover. That it is the unshared areas of our lives that Jesus is not Lord of; those things that remain unconfessed before God and others. So, repenting of our sins should involve not just us and God, but also other Christians whom we love and trust (James 5:16). And in order to break the habits of addiction, we may very well need to make practical amends for our sin. This might involve writing a letter of confession to someone from whom we've stolen; the destruction of that pile of pornographic magazines or occult books we have in our bedroom; the ripping up of the video card which we use to get those less than helpful videos, the removal of that unhelpful website from our computer's 'Favourites' file ...

A WILL DENTED BY PASSIVITY

Have a look at Hebrews 12:1–4; it's clear that there is nothing in the Christian life which is passive. While you can never earn your salvation – it comes as a gift from God through His grace – it remains true that it is down to us to 'work out our salvation' (Phil. 2:12) in active co-operation with God. That's why the verb in Romans 8:28 is a very active one, which more properly means that God *works* together with those who are called according to His purposes, to make all things good, even the bad things! There used to be a phrase around a little while ago that said 'let go and let God!' Basically it's unbiblical! We need to work things out together with God, not sit on our backsides! Receiving from God is right and biblical. But even receiving is an active attitude; receptivity and passivity are not the same.

And so Hebrews 12 talks about *throwing* off sin, *running* with perseverance, *fixing* our eyes, *considering* Jesus, and *struggling* against or *resisting* sin – all of which are active verbs! But there may be things in our lives which can easily lead us into passivity, and that will therefore impair our will. Remember, it's only a short step from an impaired will to an addiction. So, what will breed passivity?

PASSIVITY AND FALSE RELIGIONS

Any involvement in Eastern religions (other than Christianity!) or in yoga or martial arts will tend to make you passive in your reactions. A philosophy basic to most Eastern religions is that the more passive you can become, and the more you can empty your mind and look inward into some kind of spiritual vacuum, the easier it will be for you to find the god within you. This is biblically a nonsense, and it is also very dangerous, since not only nature but the spiritual world abhors a vacuum. If you empty yourself, then something (either God or Satan) will fill you! You should only 'empty yourself' in order to be filled with the Holy Spirit, which can be done only through confession, repentance and meditating on God, His Word and His self-revelation in nature. Yoga, which many view simply as a form of physical relaxation (and, some would add, of mental meditation), is actually a form of Eastern worship, and is designed to invoke spirit forces within you. Never mind that some church halls hire themselves out to yoga classes – you'd do well to have none of it! There are enough godly methods of relaxation, meditation and physical exercise!

And similarly with martial arts: I was a proponent of martial arts for some years, gaining various belts in Ju-jitsu and Okinawan Karate-Do (Goju-riu style). Not only is it unhelpful in the kingdom of God (who is a God of peace) to learn how to kill and maim people, but most martial arts are also based around harnessing spirit forces within you (Kiai) which you learn in a temple (Dojo) under the guidance of a guru (Sensei). Many martial arts sessions will involve a period of quiet or meditation to help with the training. Again, this is dangerous territory and quite different from Christian biblical meditation.

PASSIVITY AND DRUG ABUSE

Any involvement in drug abuse can also lead to passive states – physically, relationally, volitionally, emotionally, mentally and spiritually. There are links between drugs and the occult (the same word is used for both, and has its roots in the New Testament word '*pharmakeia*'). This doesn't mean that every time you take paracetamol you are in danger of demonic interference, or even of addiction! But the links between drug abuse, passivity, the occult and addiction are clear and observable; many, many drug addicts are also involved in the occult, as an inherent part of their addiction.

PASSIVITY AND 'QUE SERA, SERA' THEOLOGY

You might be thinking at this stage that you've never been involved in any Eastern religion, or in yoga, martial arts or any form of drug abuse. And so you would never have a will dented by passivity. Well, that may be true. However, there is a more subtle way that you and I can be trapped into passivity. That is through what I would call 'Que Sera, Sera' theology! You probably don't remember that song by Doris Day? – 'Que Sera, Sera'. It means 'What will be, will be'. And I know many Christians who, through wrong teaching, have adopted a kind of 'Que Sera, Sera' theology. Their view is 'if it happens, then it must have been meant to happen', and that somehow it is *all* contained (the good, the bad and the ugly!) in the sovereign, but highly mysterious, will of God! There was a great TV sketch featuring comedian Alexei Sayle, in which he jumped, leapt, twisted, contorted, gyrated and flung himself down a street, dressed in a black suit with a placard pinned on it, which said 'God'! As he went past two women, one turned to the other and said, 'That was God, wasn't it?' and the other replied, 'Yes He does move in mysterious ways, doesn't He?' I'm convinced that a lot of Christians think that the real God is equally bizarre!

Now God's ways *are* higher than our ways, and His ways are *not* our ways (Isa. 55:9). But He is *also* a God who makes Himself known; He is reasonable (Isa. 1:18) – not least so that we can learn about Him, know Him and recognise Him! God is also sovereign, but that doesn't mean that like a tyrant in a tantrum He always gets His way immediately. That's clear from Scripture, where we're told that God is unwilling for any to perish because they don't know Him (2 Pet. 3:9); and that God wants to heal everyone (Matt. 6:10; Rev. 7:16–17; 21:3–4). And yet people do perish because they don't know God, and not everyone is healed. There are many things that happen on this earth that go contrary to the will of God, because on this earth we're involved in the final stages of cosmic conflict between two expansionist kingdoms: the kingdom of God and the kingdom of Satan. So, although God will ultimately get His way, there are many occasions at the moment where He doesn't yet have His way.

If I'm right, this means that there is no place for 'Que Sera, Sera' theology, for a kind of Christian fatalism. Instead it means that we are to be actively involved in the working out of our salvation with God, not accepting the things which are clearly not of His kingdom here on earth, either in our lives, in the lives of our friends or in the lives of our communities. This kind of active warfare theology demands a will unimpaired by fatalistic theology.

PASSIVITY AND NEGATIVE SELF-IMAGE

This is another major cause of passivity. You might have

swallowed some unbibilical teaching which says that that part of your personality which is wrong, or that aspect of your physical appearance which you simply don't like, is 'the cross you have to bear'. You might be saying to yourself, 'Well, I can't help it, that's just me, it's the way I am.' Not so! If you have a bad self-image, the good news is that it can be healed.

If I'm describing you, why not check out Chapter 3 again and do the biblical thing, which is to love yourself. Get a real grip of the fact that while you're not responsible for the actions of other people towards you, you are responsible for your reactions to them. You might have been bullied and mocked at school, but if that makes you full of resentment and bitterness in your life, then make no mistake, bitterness is what you will later reap (Gal. 6:7). You are responsible under those circumstances for extending forgiveness towards your opponents, rather than bitterness. But if you constantly flip into self-pity, or the old excuse 'that's just me', then you will quickly end up in passivity, with an impaired will.

PASSIVITY AND THE MEDIA

Compact discs, tapes, films, videos, TV; all of these things at some level encourage us to be passive, rather than active; to switch into the 'switch off' mode, and vegetate in front of the TV or sound system! A word of warning – don't do it all the time. If you do, you could be heading for addiction and an impaired will. Why else do some Christians have such a hard time finding the 'off' button? There is a time to relax in front of a good video. There is a time to surround yourself in a sea of your favourite music. But there is also a time for silence. Or a time to get involved in family activities. Or a time to read a good novel, or the Bible – to be active, not passive.

DEALING WITH PASSIVITY

Of course, the opposite of passivity is activity. So the solution to 'reinflating' a will dented by passivity is to involve yourself in action. Over-activity, where you end up a driven person, is as much an addiction as anything else, but it's still true, as someone once said, 'If you want to be active for God, find out what He's doing and join in!' Even if you make mistakes, or make the wrong decision; it's better to make a wrong decision than no decision at all, as God can more easily direct a moving object than a stationary one! And action means taking one step at a time. The headlights on a car don't illuminate its destination, but only the immediate road ahead. And so it is with God's guiding of us, it's a step, not a stop; action not passivity!

David had quite a neat trick, demonstrated in Psalm 103, of speaking firmly to his own soul and stirring it up, telling it what it will do. We could do worse, because we must learn to live from our spirit and not from our body or our soul, which will sometimes betray us into passivity. Reading books, listening to tapes, studying the Bible (with a concordance and notes), keeping a journal, entering up a prayer diary, carrying around a memory book of verses and promises which are important to us – all of these things will help us to be active and not passive.

After all, our role model is Jesus. First grab hold of how good Jesus is at 'being' before 'doing', at identity before function. But then note: in all the Gospels there is only one occasion where it is said that He was asleep. It's not because He only slept once in three years, but rather that the emphasis of His work was on activity and not passivity! That's why Jesus constantly prompted responses/action from people with

His questions. It may seem a silly question to ask a man who was obviously blind what it was that he wanted from Jesus (Mark 10:51), but Jesus was trying to prompt an honest and active response from Bartimaeus. It is easy to overlook the active faith response that was demanded from the lepers in Luke 17:14, because it was only *as they went* that they were healed. So again, be active, not passive. Rest is essential; it is a creation (pre-Fall) principle (Gen. 2:2–3), and it combats drivenness. But, rest is not passive – it's actually a spiritual discipline (have a look at Chapter 10).

A WILL DENTED BY A DOMINATED/CRUSHED LIFESTYLE

Negative words (which have the same effect as curses) constantly spoken over you, parents with too high an expectation of you, or projected parental hopes, dreams and ambitions which they never fulfilled in their own lives; all of these things can dominate or crush your will. It need not be your parents. Bullies or even friends at school can do exactly the same thing, as can teachers. I remember being hauled out in front of a class and made to repeat after my teacher 'I am a dolt!' It may sound like nothing, but the power of words is enormous, and it was like a curse to me, which actually had to be prayed through very much later on.

Suddenly finding out that you weren't a planned child, but rather that your conception was an 'accident', can have a similar effect on you. Or that your parents actually wanted a little girl/boy but instead got you! All of these things can pull down your personal self-worth and will go some way towards crushing your will. Consistent isolation and rejection will do the same thing; or being manipulated by an extremely possessive or dominant family, parents, friends, or even church leaders. It impairs your ability to think, act and take responsibility for yourself, and your will becomes subject to another's.

POSITIVE CONFESSION

But your will can be re-engaged through a process of prayer and positive confession, agreeing with God about *His* will for your life, and *His* view of you, which is positive, not negative. Proverbs 6:2 talks about people who are 'trapped by what they say, ensnared by the words of their mouth', and Proverbs 16:23 says that it's a 'wise man's heart' that 'guides his mouth, and his lips promote instruction'. If this is true, then we ought to be careful what negatives about ourselves we confess from our mouths! We must make sure that we are agreeing with God and choosing the positive, not the negative. Deuteronomy 30 is very clear in the choice which God puts before us; we can choose either death and cursing, or life and blessing.

God Himself demonstrates the power of positive words. In Genesis 1 He creates by the simple act of speaking ('And God said ... and there was ...'). Similarly, in Mark 4:39, Jesus stills a storm by the power of His spoken words ('Quiet! Be still!' – and it was!). And in Mark 1:41, Jesus heals a leper by the power of His words ('Be clean!' – and he was!). The teaching to back up this demonstration is given later by Jesus in Mark 11:23, where He says whoever 'does not doubt in his heart, but believes that what he says will happen, it will be done for him'.

A WILL DENTED BY REBELLION

It is interesting that in the Bible, the sin of rebellion is closely linked to the sin of witchcraft, and that in turn is linked to the sin of domination and manipulation. (Have a look at 1 Samuel 15:22–23.) Rebellion was, after all, the original cause of Satan's fall and was rooted in pride. Rebellion hardens your will against God, and therefore weakens it towards Satan. Ultimately and fundamentally, all rebellion is a refusal of intimacy with God.

But, more subtly, rebellion can also come from a root of fear, instead of pride. You can see this in Numbers 14:7–9. Here's how it works. Fear works actively against faith. Now, faith will direct your will towards God. So fear will misdirect your will away from God, either into despair, or into false trust in yourself. You know that's happened when you find yourself thinking, 'It won't happen unless I make it happen' or 'I have been let down so many times, I'll do it myself this time'. Now, if your will is misdirected in this way, so that you are trusting only in yourself and looking after 'number one', then this is clearly rebellion against God, but born this time of fear instead of pride.

CHECK IT OUT!

Here, then, is a list of symptoms you might identify within yourself if you have a problem with a rebellious (and therefore impaired) will.

Unteachability: this can often come across as a kind of 'I know better than you' attitude.

Conceit: the 'I can *do* better' attitude. Closely linked to *Superiority:* which is the 'I *am* better' attitude.

Bitterness and Resentment: can often lead to rebellion because the thinking behind it is 'You hurt or scared me, now it's my turn!' And so you rebel against that individual, perhaps a parent, teacher or friend.

Stubbornness: this is the attitude of 'No I won't do it, and if

I have to I'll do it in my own time, in my own way!' In Proverbs 22:15 the actual word stubbornness is translated 'folly' or 'foolishness'. That's because the Hebrew word for 'a fool' is the same as the word for 'a rebel', or one who is stubborn. Please note that one of the cures in Proverbs 22:15 for rebellion and stubbornness is discipline! It might also be worth bearing in mind that the Greek word for a fool (*'moros'*, from which we get the word 'moron') means to act without counsel, in rebellion. So, in short, a rebel is a stubborn fool! Rebellion is often an attempt to establish kudos and identity outside the context of loving and serving God and others.

Possessiveness: often comes out of rebellion, where it comes across as a 'This area is mine, so keep out' attitude.

Dominance: can be a clear symptom of a rebellious will and comes across as a 'do as I say' attitude.

Manipulation: forcing people to choose sides (usually yours). This will manifest itself as a 'join my side' attitude.

Hostility: often comes across as 'keep clear of me'.

All of these symptoms can be terribly difficult to deal with in our lives, because rebellion means that at heart we aren't open to persuasion by others, whereas the Bible teaches us that we are to be submitted to one another (Eph. 5:21). The original Greek word (*hupotassein*) means 'to be open to persuasion'.

DEALING WITH REBELLION

But of course, rebellion is sin and can be dealt with as such through repentance, confession and cleansing. Saying sorry *isn't* repentance. Remorse (which simply means we're sorry we got found out) *isn't* repentance. Repentance is a change of mind leading to a change of heart and of direction; because sin is not a weakness; sin is not a simple inconvenience to the flow of our lives. We must learn to treat sin as an enemy. Sin will destroy us if we let it. And sin, passivity, a dominated or crushed lifestyle and a rebellious attitude will all dent our will, which is what Satan is after.

GETTING GOD-CENTRED

Saying 'No' and overcoming rebellion means developing God-centredness in our lives. Here are five Bible references to help you develop God-centredness.

1. Proverbs 23:7: 'For as he thinks in his heart, so is he' (NKJV). Every sinful, addictive action started life first as a thought, which made an appeal to your will – will you choose right or wrong? Therefore, be convinced of the importance of your thought-life and of your will.

2. Romans 12:1–2: Being a living sacrifice, which is your spiritual worship, is the best way to renew and transform your mind. A living sacrifice means daily decisions at the time, not living off promises for the future.

3. 2 Corinthians 10:5: Learn to 'take captive every thought to make it obedient to Christ'. This is like putting a little 'delay loop' on your mind, so you've thought about what you're thinking about *before* you speak or act on it! It's a habit that you can get into. Every good communicator thinks about what he says before he says it. If good communicators can, then so can good disciples!

4. Ephesians 6:17: Becoming God-centred is a battle for the mind. The helmet of salvation is to protect the mind that God has given you – so put it on! Significantly, a Roman helmet (the image that Paul, writer to the Ephesians, had

in mind) protected the ears (hearing) and eyes (seeing) as well as the head (thinking) and the back of the neck (attacks from behind where you least expect it).

5. James 4:7: (1) Submit yourself to God, (2) resist the devil, and you will find that (3) he must flee from you. But in every area of your life, submission is positive and active. Don't make the mistake of letting Jesus be Lord of your church or student cell, but not Lord of your fantasy life! Don't let Him be Lord of your course work, but not Lord of your spending. The answer? Submit!

OK, so re-engaging the will isn't just a matter of gritting your teeth and trying harder to overcome sin, passivity, domination or rebellion! It's a matter of repentance, of activity, of positive confession and of developing God-centredness. But once the will is re-engaged as God always intended it to be, what are the steps we can take to stay free?

BREAKING THE CYCLE

It's important to know the difference between sin in your life and problems in your life. For too long the evangelical Church has been desperately repenting of its problems, and trying to overcome its sins, which is entirely the wrong way round. What we should be doing is repenting of our sins, and overcoming our problems. So first determine whether you're dealing with a problem (enemy captivity) or a sin (enemy activity, which you've embraced).

Jesus knew the difference between the two. In Luke 13:11–16, He healed a woman by rebuking demonic activity, rather than simply praying for physical healing. In Luke 4:33–44, Jesus rebukes demons that are causing some sickness, but on other occasions He simply heals people. You see both aspects of this ministry of Jesus in His stated manifesto in Luke 4:14–19. Healing and deliverance go side by side. And Jesus passed on this same mandate in Matthew 10:1–8, so it is important that we grow in understanding the difference between sin, problems and the demonic as well.

So, at the end of this chapter, one final list! A list which you can use, be it sin, problem or demons that you're dealing with!

1. Believe in your head and your heart that God is good, and that His will for you is also good (Rom. 12:2).
2. Believe that you are responsible for your actions and reactions, though not for the actions of people towards you (Gal. 5:1).
3. Believe that freedom *is* actually possible.
4. Deal with the root (causes), and not just the fruit (symptoms). Make a clean break from the past, deliberately not leaving yourself any little bolthole just in case you fancy nipping back into the sin, problem, captivity later on. Ruthlessly leave no provision for defeat. Have a look at Matthew 5:29–30; Acts 19:17–19; Romans 13:14.
5. Admit your feelings (as we saw Jesus do in Matthew 26:38) and in doing so seek the support of your friends around you. Recognise that you are still close to God, even in the middle of the turmoil of your feelings.
6. Accept that you may need prayer from those whom you love and trust, who are more mature in Jesus than you, so you can be set free from demonic interference.
7. Deal ruthlessly with all future temptation. Use the *reckon-resist-replace* method outlined on pages 136–137). But don't fight temptation on your own – rather, fight it with a transparent life and with the

support of those around you. And it might help you to note that there are many occasions in the Bible where people fell, only to get up again. So you might want to make a mental note of verses like Psalm 37:23–24; Proverbs 24:16; Jeremiah 8:4; Micah 7:8. They're encouraging!

Well, there you have it. Forgive yet another list, but I did want to be practical. Demonic influence and activity in our lives is not uncommon. Satan's kingdom, like God's, is expansionist, and is always looking to take territory in my life and yours. The bottom line is this: Who will be boss? Will you rule over your own desires in submission to Jesus? Or will you let Satan? My hope is that this and the previous chapter will help you move forward into more of the freedom for which Christ came to set you free.

Chapter 7

'MALE AND FEMALE HE CREATED THEM ...'

You must have noticed how much of creation around you reflects the redemptive order of God? It's not just an issue of the beauty of sun-tinged feathered clouds at the end of a summer's day, or the magnificent grandeur of a Scottish mountain reflected in the depths of a loch, that reveals God to us through His creation. It is also something to do with the many analogies drawn from nature that we find in Scripture. Whether it's Jesus as the Lion of Judah, or as the Lamb of God who takes away the sins of the world, or whether it is the children of God who get up on wings like eagles (Rev. 5:5; John 1:29; Isa. 40:31), both Scripture and nature are full of God imaging Himself to people, who in turn stand alone and unique at the peak of His creation, made in His image. But that image is tarnished in you and me. War has crept in between sexes. These next two chapters take a look at how radical holiness demands a radical reappraisal of the relationship between men and women.

PLAN 'A'

In the story which explains the purpose of creation (found in

Genesis 1:27–28), we find that God gives the role of imaging Himself/showing Himself to the rest of the created order as a joint role which goes *equally* to man and to woman. The fulfilment of the role, nothing less than the imaging of God to creation, can only be possible in their partnership together. What's more, God's mandate to steward and tend the earth also goes jointly to men and to women. It is the disruption and destruction of this imaging of God by humanity into the created order, which becomes the primary target of satanic activity. So by Genesis 3:16 there is conflict between men and women as a result of their fall into wilful sin. This conflict can be typified as men dominating over women, and women manipulating men. Consequent fear, suspicion and pain cause further alienation between the sexes, leading to greater mis-understanding, stereotyping and even to structural sexism.

PLAN 'B'

The salvation/wholeness which Jesus came to bring is so much wider than the forgiveness of our sins! It includes repentance of the sins of our gender, embracing the redeemed strengths of our gender, giving and receiving forgiveness of the opposite gender, and growing in understanding and partnership with them. All of this is an integral outworking of the salvation which Jesus has bought us. The journey towards reconciliation, which is the hope of redemption (Gal. 3:28), needs to be both an individual and corporate journey. You and I must embark on it *in* us, before we can embark on it *through* us in our relationships with members of the opposite sex.

EXPLORING THE DIFFERENCES!

Because both men and women are created in the image of God and as such reflect God in different ways, it does become important to explore and understand the distinctives. The biological distinctives are obvious! Women have breasts and a vagina. Men have a penis and testes. When it comes to definition the sexual definitions are the easiest to deal with. We're dealing with biology, built around hormones, chromosomes, physiology, genes, anatomy, differences in muscle weight and so on. This is to do with maleness and femaleness, means of reproduction; the differences are recognised everywhere, there is a universality about the characteristics of maleness and femaleness.

Yet it seems inconsistent with the holistic Jewish view of humanity that the only difference between the sexes is biological. Indeed, it's clear that when God talks about humanity imaging Him, He isn't talking about us looking like Him physically, as God is spirit (John 4:24). So, male and female must reflect His image in some other way. It is this gender identity which is less easy to define. It has something to do with culture, with roles and expectations, language, lifestyle and learning. This is more about masculinity and femininity, than maleness and femaleness. Our upbringing inevitably contributes to our understanding of gender identity. It can establish gender cultures, giving us positive or negative parental role models, received both consciously and unconsciously. Our upbringing can inculcate us both with fears and confidence, and can even pass on to us aspects of generational sin harking all the way back to the fall (Gen. 3) and touched on in this book in Chapters 5 and 6 where we looked at wholeness and generational curses.

A CONTINUUM

Allowing for all of the above, it still seems that in reading through Scripture there is a recognition of certain characteristics which are more masculine than feminine, and vice versa. However, Scripture is far from rigid in separating the two. Rather, whilst we are all either physically male or female (with extremely rare genetic disorders as the exception) we will all have some of the characteristics normally associated with the other gender. In this sense masculinity and femininity are linked to, but not synonymous with, male and female. Males will be predominantly masculine in gender identity, but not exclusively so, and females likewise predominantly but not exclusively female. Having said this, it also appears from Scripture to be God's intention that we feel a peace, wholeness and a oneness with being either male and masculine, or female and feminine.

WHAT'S THE PROBLEM?

When we don't embark on a journey of redemption and reconciliation, the result can be a kind of demonic stereotyping. So we find historically both men and women have argued both ways as to the superiority and inferiority of the other gender. Or have made the mistake of approaching the genders as though they were literally from different planets. (See John Gray's book, *Men are from Mars, Women are from Venus.*) Sometimes, in striving for equality, both genders have maintained that they are identical to each other, and are therefore exactly the same in roles, functions and capacities. And some have simplistically related everything to biology and therefore to sexuality.

COMMUNICATION – AN ISSUE

Forgive a few stereotypes; let's see if we can identify elements of truth from them. Men can appear (if not actually feel on the inside) more confident to speak out their thoughts and opinions and to express them more strongly, almost always as though they are well thought through and definitive. What's more, men tend to be louder than women, with harder/deeper voices. On the other hand women may need to be encouraged to have their thoughts and opinions drawn out, given space to make the most of the opportunity and not come under male intimidation. Tending to have a softer/higher voice can make it harder to be heard among the male voices, and can lead to greater apprehension in feeding back perspectives. Women tend to come to their own opinions by talking them through and generally being more openly persuadable. Perhaps, as a rule of thumb, women are frequently found to apologise more often. It might be helpful to look at some examples, not only of *how* things might be said, but also *what*.

YOU'LL BE SORRY YOU SAID THAT ...

If you're a guy I'd be surprised if you can't relate to some of the following statements often made by men in the context of relationships, teamwork, family ...

- You shouldn't worry so much.
- But that's not what I said.
- OK I am sorry.
- Now can we just forget about it.
- But we *do* talk.
- That's not what I meant.
- How can you say that?

- Last week we spent the whole day together!
- OK just forget it.
- All right I'll wash the dishes.
- Does that make you happy?
- Look, there's nothing we can do about it.
- If you're just going to complain about doing it, then just don't do it.
- All right then, you can do it from now on.

Similarly, I'd be surprised if as a woman you can't relate to some of the following:

- You work too hard, you should take a day off.
- You should call a plumber – he'll know what to do.
- Don't put that there.
- You want to spend time with your friends? What about me?
- There is a parking space over there, just turn around.
- Why don't you stop and ask for directions?
- I didn't know where you were.
- You're not leaving yourself enough time.
- That shirt doesn't match those trousers.
- Pete phoned again! When are you going to phone him back?
- You should have told me that.

It's important in all of this to constantly remind ourselves that good communication is not about what is *given*, it's about what is *received*. Good communication rarely relies on one code alone. So it doesn't matter how precisely you use words, or how inexactly you use them. Alongside the words will go a whole raft of more subtle nuances; a look, a raise of the eyebrows, a toss of the head, a flashing glance, the twitching of the lips, a folding of the arms – and more. Communication is also about tone of voice as well as body language, and is as much to do with history as with the present. Communication essentially is not a means of manipulation, it is a way of letting people in on the window of our souls and into our own internal worlds. Real communication often runs at a kind of sub-strata to that which is initially given. So, it's important to read the *signals* (however they are given, in whatever codes) as well as to analyse the *content*.

TEAM DYNAMIC – AN ISSUE

Team dynamic is affected by the balance of men and women on a team as well as their positive and negative gender distinctives. We've all 'teamed it' at some stage. Team could be a class at school, or a seminar at university. It could be a project delivery team at work or a worship team at church, or even the team which constitutes your family unit. Again, hopefully, some helpful team-truisms.

If there are more men in a team then often there will be more banter and joking. This will also be likely to veer towards the cutting or sarcastic edge. Men will often tell stories not so much for inclusion and mutual appreciation, as for potential exclusion and the purposes of 'topping' the story just related previously. Male dominated teams tend also to be more task-orientated. They are often less relational, with 'success' strongly defined by 'delivery'. Men will often focus more on separation and their distinctive task or role within the team context, and so often have a stronger focus on 'self'. And guys will worry more about 'rights' and be more prepared to adopt confrontational attitudes to solve problems. Men are also more comfortable with hierarchies that clearly differentiate one from another. For these reasons men can sometimes live their lives compartmentalised into neatly identifiable 'boxes' (eg work, family, social, father, husband, church, etc) and communicate (or not!) accordingly.

Where there are more women in a team, the team will tend to be more intimate, closer in relationship, with affection more readily shown and will be more people/team focused. John Adair, a team management consultant, proposed that the three vital constituents for a successful team are as follows[1]:

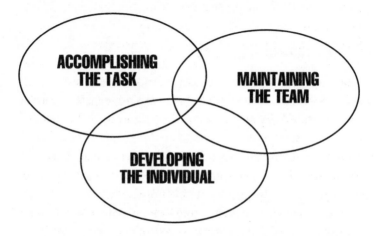

Adair maintained that the best teams gave equal focus to all three constituent parts. From the above analysis you will see that men would predominate in focusing on Accomplishing the Task, whereas women would focus on Maintaining the Team. Both would tend to show an equal focus on Developing the Individual, but for different reasons. The women would tend to be equally concerned about the development of each individual, where the men would be primarily concerned in developing themselves.

In the team context women would also tend to focus on connectedness, one to another, and on interdependence, with a clear focus on others rather than on themselves, and with a tendency to worry more about 'responsibilities' than rights. Where men will confront to solve problems, women will tend to emphasise care and protection, and be more comfortable with network organisations where inclusiveness is the aim, rather than with hierarchies.

In my own experience, awareness of these potential issues is half the battle to combatting them! When we first launched DNA, the church-based year-long discipleship programme, the DNA Team then consisted of three men and one woman. I honestly think it must have taken us the best part of a year to begin to understand the extent of gender differences, on both sides. Ness had to learn to appreciate the fun and non-vindictiveness of male humour! We had to recognise its excesses and combative edge, and rein it back accordingly. We had to learn to be less focused on the task at hand and more focused on how we delivered what we delivered, and how we cared for one another in the process. Ness had to embrace an emphasis on delivery, because under the hand of God we had a task to perform which gave us a reason to be a team together and sometimes meant taking time out from the more personal 'touchy-feely' moments. Some of these lessons were learned instinctively. But many of them were learned through honest, open, frank discussion and debate, usually at the end of a long working day over a pint in a local pub! What we (and you?) were after was the recognised need for balance, where goals are achieved, people are cared for and mutually developed. Where humour is inclusive, and not exclusive – for appreciation, and not for put down. Where together as a team we were giving to, learning from and shaping one another. Where distinctives were not only recognised, but actively encouraged and appreciated.

HISTORY – AN ISSUE

I hinted earlier that our communication across the genders was often impacted by our histories together. Let's unpack that some more. Because of structural, institutional and generational sin, it's probably the case that the majority of men are used to working in an all male, or predominantly male environment. There's a real need for both genders to learn how to work in a new set up. If a guy has always been in an all-male team, it's a good exercise to put himself into an all-female team (even if as a deliberate exercise and for a limited period of time). This will give the guy a taster of how it feels to be in an unfamiliar scenario, with unfamiliar ways of operating. What's more, he should realise that most of the time that's the way most women have to operate, as a minority gender in many teams. If you want to wise up on the history of the conflict between men and women, you may find the following truisms helpful:

LIES/CONDITIONING ABOUT WOMEN	FACTS ABOUT WOMEN AND MEN
Women are illogical.	Women and men are equally logical
Women are intuitive.	More than 80% of intuitive information is correct. Women and men demonstrate equal intuitive ability.
Women are weak.	Women have greater physical endurance than men, greater energy reserves, adapt better to extremes of temperature, survive accidents more often and survive starvation, exposure, fatigue, shock and illness better than men, and they live longer.

LIES/CONDITIONING ABOUT WOMEN	FACTS ABOUT WOMEN AND MEN
Women are unreliable with money.	Family finances are run successfully more often by women than by men (indications from the Old Testament agree – Prov. 31:10–22). Before sexist conditioning takes root, the reality is that girls score higher in maths than boys of the same age.
Women are indecisive.	In the home and workplace women make more decisions than men, women's ability to consult widely produces better executive decisions.
Women cause unbidden sexual feelings in men	Men choose to embrace sexual feelings and can decide not to.
Women are too emotional.	People who have easy access to their emotions think more clearly and see from more perspectives (emotional intelligence). Male and female babies show no difference in their ability or tendency to cry. Social conditioning?
A woman's main goal in life is to be loved by a man.	Women and men both need to be loved and to love, and to contribute to society.
Women cannot lead.	Women lead all day, every day. Women's interactive thinking can make them particularly good leaders.

THE BIBLE – AN ISSUE

Unfortunately, over the years the Bible itself has often been used as an excuse to perpetuate gender wars, in particular in the oppression of women. Bad exegesis (the understanding of why, how and to whom Scripture was written at the time) and appalling hermenuetics (the application of Scripture to the present) and sometimes basic (or even wilful) mis-translation by predominantly male translators, have all contributed to a distortion of God's Word when it comes to the subject of women and men relating and working together. It is a huge issue, and one worthy of further study and application, but for now, a few headlines.

KINGDOM AUTHORITY

Can women biblically exercise authority? According to the Bible, kingdom authority is the authority to serve people (Mark 10:42–45). So the real question about women in leadership and ministry is, 'Are women allowed to lay down their lives for others, if they know a calling to know, love, serve and invest into a group of people?' This is not a gender issue about who can rule, which is a worldly model of leadership, but about who can have authority to *serve*. Secular feminism centres around gaining equal rights; biblical feminism centres around gaining equal rights to serve.

The Bible also makes it clear that any authority which women *or* men exercise is not authority over people, but rather over the enemy and his activities (Luke 10:18). This kind of authority comes from our position in Christ, which is open to both women and men and does not come from our gender.

What's more, according to Luke 7:1–10, kingdom authority

flows from being in submission. There is therefore no such thing as a one-man, or one-woman ministry. Biblical leadership is team leadership. You cannot lead effectively if you don't know how to be led. This leads us nicely on to the next point.

Ephesians 5:21 is a biblical command for *mutual* submission as a value of the kingdom. This is a command for *all* believers, irrespective of gender. It's worth noting that spheres of authority (for example to do with government, work, church, family and so on) are independent of each other. Authority in one sphere cannot automatically be transferred over into another. What does this mean in practice? A man might be an elder of his local church, but work on a business team where the project manager is a woman. And vice versa.

The biblical evidence for authority, servanthood, leadership and ministry being open to both genders goes right the way back to Genesis. Check it out for yourself:

- In Genesis 1:26 it was both male and female who ruled.
- In Genesis 1:27 they were both created in His image.
- In Genesis 1:28 they were both blessed and it was to both of them that God spoke.

As we've already seen, it's in the coming together of male and female that the image of God is revealed. All the qualities and attributes of maleness and femaleness are found in the Godhead itself. That's why there are references to God as both Father and Mother (Isa. 66:13; Matt. 6:9; Luke 13:34). In God's economy with words, might it not be significant that the Hebrew word in the Old Testament for Holy Spirit (*Ruach*) is a feminine word? Similarly the word 'helper', which is used to describe the woman's relationship to the man, is also used (indeed more frequently – 15 times in the Old Testament) to describe God Himself; it does *not* denote inferiority. Rather, it describes how man's deficiency was to be made up so that he could be complete. In the same way God helps us to make up for our deficiencies. So He too is referred to as a 'Helper'. And so perhaps as you might expect, there is no aspect of life, ministry, authority and servanthood in the Old Testament, from which women are excluded in God's purposes, and all of that expressed in leadership, in the prophetic, in government, in worship and in family life. Indeed, in Proverbs 31:16–18, 24, the 'ideal' woman is actually a business woman. Other examples include Miriam (Micah 6:4), Deborah (Judg. 4), and Huldah (2 Chron. 34:14–28).

ENTER JESUS!

Part of Jesus' success in imaging humanity as it *should* be is a deliberate and proactive raising of the status of women. In Matthew 5:27–30, Jesus firmly places the responsibility for the way men view women onto the men. Jewish culture insisted the women be segregated and cover their hair and faces in public, but Jesus clearly teaches that the man is responsible for his own attitude and behaviour towards women. Women no longer become sexual objects, but people of equal value. Jesus even reinterpreted and changed the provision of the law so that women could divorce men. Previously only the men were allowed to initiate divorce, and could do so on a mere whim (a burnt dinner for example!). But Jesus made it much harder for men to institute divorce proceedings, whilst at the same time upholding God's ideal for lifelong committed marriage (Matt. 5:31–32). In addition Jesus radicalised the meaning of adultery to include even the mental act of dehumanising women. Unlike other rabbis of His day, Jesus had female disciples in the group that followed Him around and benefited from His teaching. In

Luke 10:39 we see Mary 'sitting at the feet' of Jesus, a technical term for being a disciple (see how Paul refers to his teacher Gamaliel in Acts 22:3, NRSV). Women travelled with Jesus (Mary, Joanna, Susanna). Some of them came from Galilee and followed Him as far as Jerusalem, and were present at the time of His death. Jesus even allowed Himself to be financially dependent on some of His wealthier female disciples (Luke 8:1–3). In Luke 11:27 the woman in the crowd cries out, 'Blessed is the mother who gave you birth and nursed you' because her culture had taught her that a woman's primary role and value was dependent on bearing children, and male children at that! Jesus' immediate reply showed how much He disliked that concept, and in one sentence He makes the role and value of women equal to that of men, ie based upon the will of God and obedience, 'Blessed rather are those who hear the word of God and obey it.'

Where other rabbis of the day would deliberately avoid referring to women (even praying 'I thank God I am not a woman or a dog'!), Jesus, in contrast, frequently used women as examples in His stories (Luke 13:20–21; 15:8–10; 18:1–8; 21:1–4). The story of the woman caught in adultery (John 8:1–11) sees Jesus restoring the dignity of women even in the condition of sin (a sin, incidentally, shared by her male partner!), and in Luke 13:10–17, Jesus creates a previously unknown title for a woman crippled for 18 years by calling her a '*Daughter* of Abraham'. This is to bestow upon her full membership of the covenant community in her own right (the term 'Son of Abraham' was well known, and re-emphasised a man's worth); so Jesus not only dealt with her physically, but also healed and restored to her a sense of dignity and self-worth. Two of the longest conversations recorded in the Gospels were with women – Jesus was happy to have long theological conversations with them and treated them as responsible people. To a Samaritan woman He uniquely reveals Himself as the Messiah (John 4:26). To a Syro-Phoenician woman He engages in banter and debate (Mark 7:26–30). In a culture where a woman was not allowed to touch any man other than her husband, Jesus was happy to be touched by women and to touch them in return. He even allowed a woman who was probably a prostitute 'to wipe away the tears with her uncovered hair', which culturally was seen as a method of sexual stimulation, but which Jesus here, seeing the heart behind it, re-interprets. It was a group of women who stayed with Jesus right through to the crucifixion, when most of the men had fled. It was to women that Jesus revealed the most momentous miracle in human history when He was resurrected. It was to them that He gave the task of telling others, and that in a culture and society, where a woman's testimony was not even valid in court! Enough said?

Perhaps it's because Jesus is the total and perfect model of redeemed masculinity that He deliberately began to break down the stereotypes, by fulfilling what were traditionally seen to be women's roles. So we find Jesus cooking breakfast for His friends (John 21:9), cuddling children on His lap (Mark 9:36; 10:16), washing His disciples' feet (John 13:5), and openly expressing His emotions. The only description that He ever gave of Himself has a distinct gender bias towards the feminine, 'I am gentle and humble in heart' (Matt. 11:29). Perhaps this is the best explanation we get as to why Jesus came as a man, perhaps to 'image the powerful, empowering the powerless' (or as Luke 4:18 puts it, 'to release the oppressed').

But of all the authors in Scripture, and of all passages which might be used to interpret restrictive roles for women, it is the apostle Paul who is the most used and abused. When we grapple with the so-called 'difficult' passages, there are at least five principles we must take on board.

1. We need to have the right exegesis (context) and hermeneutics (application) and not simply filter things through our own prejudices.
2. We need to read unclear text in the light of clear text.
3. We need to understand the historical and cultural issues prevalent at the time.
4. We ought to recognise that teaching texts take precedence over corrective texts. The latter tend to deal with specific situations where things were going wrong, and it is always a mistake to draw a generality from a specific, rather than the other way round.
5. We should recognise that Paul (an ultimate pragmatic) didn't always tie in his practice with his doctrine. He would occasionally embrace the unnecessary in order to see Jesus exalted and the gospel promoted. An example of this would be Paul's teaching that converted Gentiles did not need to be circumcised, followed by his circumcision of the unfortunate Gentile Timothy!

So in the light of this, how do we interpret the following:

1 CORINTHIANS 11:2–16

Corinth was the New Testament equivalent of present-day Thailand! There, the sex industry underpinned society. In that culture, at that time, full, loose and uncovered hair was a focus of sexual attraction, and was as provocative as going 'topless' would be in our Western culture. On the other hand, head covering was a sign of a married woman's honour and dignity, much like a modern wedding ring. *Not* to have your head covered as a woman was a sign of a prostitute's availability. It was in this context that, because of the gospel of liberation, women had begun to learn that they were equal to men. However, they were taking their freedom too far, throwing off their head coverings and therefore not being culturally sensitive or helpful to the unsaved men of that culture. And so, in an attempt to avoid mixed messages being sent out, and because Paul wants the women to stand out as being different for the *right* reasons (as anointed women of God), he is at pains to stress that there should be no hint of sexual immorality in the community of God's people, which represents redeemed humanity.

Paul wants marriage to be honoured and women to dress appropriately *in that context*, whilst at the same time placing no restriction, for example, on praying out loud or prophesying. The application for us is simple. Marriage is to be respected. The symbol of a wedding ring is to be honoured, women are to be respected and stand out as being different for the *right* reasons in our culture, and not the wrong reasons. (A gospel of freedom doesn't mean Christian women should parade topless down the High Street, for example.) If women are made to wear head coverings in today's Church the question is obvious; does it promote or hinder the gospel in our culture? I'd suggest it hinders it with its oppressive cultural irrelevance.

1 CORINTHIANS 14:34-35

The cultural context is simple; at this time and in this place there was a tendency for uneducated women, sitting on a different side of the church's meeting to their husbands (because of a segregationist approach), to call out to their husbands, 'What's going on?' This was obviously highly disruptive and disrespectful. The injunction that 'women should not speak' clearly already runs contrary to what we have learned in 1 Corinthians 11, where it's been established that they can pray and prophesy. The actual word that's used is not 'to preach' or 'to teach' but rather 'to chatter'. Paul wants to bring order to the meetings. A modern-day hermeneutic is obvious; this is a plea for women not to be left uneducated, but rather to be educated alongside men. And for people to cut down the chatter in public meetings, as it is distracting.

1 TIMOTHY 2:8–15

This passage finds us in Ephesus, which was renowned for a very strong Artemis/goddess cult. This cult was markedly anti-men and anti-marriage, and involved three levels of priestesses and one level of eunuchs! It is worth bearing in mind that Timothy is a young (perhaps as young as 17!) male church leader in the town. In this context, women of high social standing from the Artemis cult had got saved, but as immature Christians they were now trying to influence the church with their own values, by dressing to intimidate with jewellery and flamboyant clothing, showing off their wealth and status. They were also, in keeping with the nature of the cult, domineering and unaccountable. And so in verse 12 the word translated 'authority' is a rather remarkable one, used only once in the whole of Scripture, and it literally means to domineer, usurp, take over, or even to murder! It's clearly not acceptable for men or women to lead in such a way! Paul wants Timothy to have some latitude, or breathing space, in his leadership, and wants women to learn godly ways and values.

So Paul doesn't use the more usual and stronger word 'never' in what is actually a very *specific* prohibition of teaching or having authority. Which presumably means, once learning has been gained, this prohibition would have been revoked. That it cannot be taken as an absolute command for all women, at all times and in all contexts, is made clear by examples like Priscilla teaching Apollos (Acts 18:24–26). Nor would it have allowed Phoebe to become a deacon, Junia to become an apostle and Priscilla to become more prominent in ministry than the male Aquila (which is why her name is mentioned before his). If this were a prohibition for all women, at all times, in all contexts, then it is difficult also to understand why Paul begins a church in Philippi with women (Acts 16:13–15) when a Jewish synagogue was not allowed to be founded on women. It is actually in female Lydia's home that the church meets. Nor would Paul have referred (as he does on many occasions) to many women as co-workers (Phil. 4:2–3), which is one of Paul's favourite terms for those who work with him in the apostolic work of spreading the gospel!

Verse 15 of the Timothy passage: 'Women will be saved through child-bearing' cannot possibly be taken at face value, because otherwise it irradicates and nullifies the work of Jesus and the cross! I take it to mean that through *one* woman's specific child-bearing (Mary) people are now saved (ie through Jesus).

So the application for today is surely obvious; people should learn maturity before, out of immaturity, they seek to influence or teach others. And the worldly values of wealth and status have no influence with the Church. And that consequently leadership is based on anointing, character, servanthood (open to both genders) and not on the ability to intimidate.

WHAT DO *YOU* THINK?

I can come to no other conclusion but that for too long the

Church has limped on with one hand tied behind her back. It's not even as though we have tried to manage with only half of the Church empowered and envisioned for leadership, ministry and servanthood. The reality is that there are more women in the Church (perhaps because they respond more readily and intuitively to God than men do) than there are men. So using oppressive, restrictive practices against women renders *more* than half the Church ineffective! And yet into all of this Jesus came to set *all* of us free with a gospel of freedom. It is the gospel that does not make everyone the same, but it does make everyone equal and free. It is the gospel that breaks the yoke of oppression and restores people to their right relationships with God, with one another and with the created order. The Church, which is the bride of Christ, is a formative model of this new and redeemed humanity. It has no room for discrimination or oppression. There can be no ruling elite. We must play to one another's strengths, we must cover one another's weaknesses. We must appreciate and validate one another's differences. Male models of ministry and leadership will not suffice. We need a new understanding, with new models of working together and a new language to communicate it. Consequently, having women elders, women in ministry and servanthood is *not* an optional extra, it is *not* a matter of cultural sensitivity or political correctness. Rather it is a restoration of the original design, purposes, imaging and mandate of God. Well, that's what I think! What about you?

MODELLING

Perhaps one of the most effective models for demonstrating and nurturing the redemption of gender distinctives is that of the family. When Scripture talks about family it does not mean the

Western version of the nuclear family (mum, dad and 1.64 kids!), but rather the extended family (the Greek word '*oikos*' meaning network or household) of blood relatives and those within your immediate community. Here one of the roles of adults was to role model to children, what femininity and masculinity were. Within the Jewish family, in both Old and New Testaments, it was assumed that although these roles were the primary responsibility of the parents it was not exclusively theirs, and the wider family and community had a duty in this role as well, especially if one of the parents were dead or absent. This is in marked contrast to the fragmentation and geographical dispersion of our own modern society. It has been suggested by Leanne Payne, amongst other writers, that a part of gender distinctive is that the mother imparts an overall sense of well-being and personhood to her children, whilst the father affirms his sons and daughters in their sexual gender identity. This involves the process of mediating in the face of conflict or confusion, as well as repeated, specific instances of affirmation, spoken blessing, reassurance and demonstration.

I hope I've said enough in this chapter to encourage and challenge you in your thinking and your behaviour as a radical follower of Jesus pursuing radical holiness. None of us can do that in an individualistic way; a measure in which the kingdom has come into our lives is the way we 'do' relationships with one another, and that rightly and necessarily involves the way that women and men relate to and work with one another. And that leads us nicely on to the next chapter ...

1. John Adair, *Effective Teambuilding* (Ashgate Publishing Co., 1986).

Chapter 8

SEXUALITY

I noted in the last chapter that it was probably easier to talk in terms of maleness and femaleness than in terms of masculinity and femininity. That is certainly true in terms of biology, genetics, chromosomes and so on. Once we start to look at the gamut of human sexuality it quickly becomes obvious that hard and fast definitions are not easy to make and if we mistakenly try to determine our identity through our sexuality, then we are in as much potential difficulty as if we try to define our identity through our gender. I have been at pains again and again in this book to try to punch home one simple, overriding message; if our identity is not found first, foremost and fundamentally in Christ, then it is not to be found anywhere with any degree of security.

THE FIRST SEXUAL BEING

Nonetheless our sexuality is an essential part of our humanity and it is so because it was created by God in the first place. God is the first sexual Being; He had the first sexual thought. He created us in His image, male and female (as we have seen in the last chapter) and that included the sexual act of procreation. So, unlike some of the mistakes made by certain quarters of the Church over the years, we can affirm that sex and our sexuality is essentially good.

However, because of the Fall, the image of God in us and through us has been distorted and that includes the sexual act and all of our sexuality. It has been damaged by sin and everybody is in need of God's redeeming grace in their sexuality. This is true whether we are sexually active or inactive, married or single, hetero or homosexual in our orientation; we all come to God in a state of sexual brokenness.

The above two facts demand the next two statements. Firstly, that God has a total acceptance for us; whatever we have done, or whatever has been done to us; in terms of our sexuality, God meets us, welcomes and embraces us right where we are. Secondly, because God is a God of grace He has more than acceptance for us, there are also the riches that He bought for us at Christ's expense; God is wanting to cleanse and heal us from sexual sin and brokenness and to bring us into a place of freedom in our sexuality. So as we approach the topic of sexuality we can have total confidence in God's goodness and in His design. He is not in the business of barring us from enjoyment. He has come to give us back our lives, not take them from us, and bring life to the full, which applies as much to sex and sexuality as to anything else. To reject, resent or react against God's plan for our sexuality is to fundamentally misunderstand His desire for us, which is for good days, good deeds, and good gifts (Jer. 29:11; Matt. 5:16), and to fail to realise that every good gift comes from God in the first place (James 1:17) and that includes sex and sexuality.

SOCIETY'S VIEW

In the society which today surrounds the radical follower of Jesus Christ, sex is conveyed as the ultimate pleasure and experience. Having a fulfilled sex life is seen as a basic human right, the ultimate experience with another person; intimacy without commitment. To this extent sex has become under-valued, but over-rated. Individuals are defined ultimately and primarily by their sexuality and gender and by their sexual activity or lack of it, and the orgasm has replaced the crucifix as the meaning/symbol of salvation!

GOD'S VIEW

However, from God's perspective, people are made in His image and they are remade as a new creation and set free from the effects of sin if they choose to follow Christ. People therefore have a dignity and value, regardless of how sexually attractive they are and regardless of their sexual orientation. So while our sexuality is an integral part of us, we are far more than that and sex is not the ultimate expression of love and intimacy from God's perspective. In the economy of God's language, in the New Testament He uses three separate words to describe the nature of love.

Firstly, there is *eros* love, which is sexual love. It gives us the word erotic and pertains to sexual expression.

Secondly, there is *phileo* love, which is brotherly love, human love and a shadow of divine love. It is however both finite and potentially fickle.

Thirdly, there is *agape* love, which is divine love and actually defines God Himself ('God is Love': 1 John 4:16). This is the deepest form of love, it is covenant based and is the love which is at the very heart of God and flows out of the nature of who God is.

Now identity is not to be found from eros love – it is entirely possible to be complete and fulfilled in our day-to-day lives without eros love. But we cannot be fulfilled and complete without agape and phileo love. We need relationship with God and with one another. Similarly, marriage is only complete with all three of these kinds of love. So eros love is secondary to, and can only grow out of, agape and phileo love if it is to have any meaning deeper than the purely physical.

AND SEX IS ... ?

Well, according to Genesis 1:26–28 and Genesis 2:18–25 sex has a number of important aspects. Firstly, it is to do with imaging God Himself. There is something in male and female being joined together that images the diversity of God's personality. God is fully male and fully female and therefore best revealed when the two come together. When two people come together in such a way, they become 'one flesh', which biblically indicates very much more than simply physical union; we are talking about cleaving and uniting together at the level of spirit, soul and body.

This is one of the reasons why the Bible uses the phrase 'to know' one another with regard to sex, because it implies that the sexual act is not just physical but is a unique, emotional and spiritual bonding between two people. So the Hebrew word for cleave is '*dabaq*', which means to be joined together through sexual intercourse, and the Greek word is '*proskallao*', which means to be adhered to for purposes of deep intimacy ('*pros*' means to move forward or to go towards, whilst '*kallao*' means to glue together). So sexual union from God's perspective can be described as a blending of people's spirits and bodies face to face. (It is interesting, for example, that in the New Testament, when describing sex between animals, the only Greek word used is '*kallao*', implying that this is not an intimate act of unveiling and that it lacks the spiritual bond.

Precisely because sex is intended to be an unveiling of your very self to your spouse, there is an emotional bonding, which complements the spiritual and physical bonding. There is a spiritual exchange, which is intended to be life-enhancing, but when practised outside God's design (ie outside of monogamous life-long commitment in marriage) leads to a loss of oneself. Yet at the same time it remains deeply spiritual since there are only two kingdoms which express spiritual reality. To defy God in an act of sexual union outside of marriage means that the sexual bond is made in the kingdom of Satan, rather than the kingdom of God. John Kirkpatrick, a Christian writer, describes sex as taking a photograph of the other person with your own spirit as the film!

It may seem obvious to say (or even superfluous in an age of readily available and efficient contraception), but sex also carries with it the potential of procreation; ie the production of children! Contrary to the teaching of some aspects of the Church, it is more than this, but it certainly does include it!

Finally, in this overview of what constitutes sex, it is important to reflect that in God's view and according to Scripture, sexual activity and expression is exclusive to male and female. The one-flesh spiritual union is fundamentally about male and female being joined together and linked. This is demonstrable, not only in physical design (a penis is designed to fit into a vagina as opposed to an anus, for example), but also in terms of gender design. Only as the two different genders of humanity join together does sex, as part of marriage, reflect

God's image in the way that He fully intended.

These last statements deserve some further attention. This is because they have a direct impact on the lives of people (perhaps even you as you read this book), and people always deserve further attention. For too long the Church has had a negative and knee-jerk reaction towards people who find that their primary orientation is towards homosexuality. The reality is, as with gender expression so too with human sexuality expression. There is a complex spectrum of human sexuality and our position on that spectrum is rarely at either end of the extreme of hetero or homosexuality. Nor indeed is our position on that spectrum necessarily static. The incidences of male homosexuality amongst heterosexually-oriented individuals in prisons would tend to indicate that, at least at a superficial physical level. The debate continues to rage (sometimes long and loudly) concerning the causes of homosexual orientation. The debate divides basically between 'nature or nurture' as the predominant factor. There are those who would maintain that nature through the genetic code is the predominant factor in predetermining a person's sexual orientation, although there is no conclusive evidence that a person is born either homosexual or heterosexual, and then there are those who would maintain that it is more to do with nurture, in other words that environment is the predominant factor. The reality is that it is probably a combination of several influences, which will not necessarily affect everyone the same way all of the time. Certainly genetic make-up should not determine moral choices, and certainly emotions and sexuality are linked – sexual arousal is a sexualised emotion. Clearly our emotional/sexual development is influenced by messages that we receive from ourselves, via parents or parental role models. It is particularly the case that the same sex person is specially significant in homosexual development. A child looks for positive affirmation and security and where the same sex parent is either weak in influence or even absent that *can* have a bearing on or in sexual orientation. So too *can* emotional and/or sexual abuse. But the reality is that the development of our emotions and sexuality is as unique as a fingerprint and so each one of us is left with a unique emotional and sexual orientation.

AND GOD SAYS ... ?

It is true that each time homosexual activity is mentioned in the Bible it is done so in a negative context. However, it is also true that some of the contexts are very specific and *cannot* be applied across the board to *all* homosexual activity with any degree of exegetical integrity. For example, in Genesis 19 and Judges 19 the specific context is that of homosexual rape (*'yadha*, which means 'to know'). The issue here is of physical activity born out of abuse, not love, and therefore is not very relevant to the potential expression of a committed, loving homosexual relationship. Even though the city of Sodom has lent its name to a form of homosexual activity, it is fair to recognise that there were many other sins connected to that city as well as those of homosexual activity (Ezek. 16:48–49).

The message of Leviticus 18:22 and 20:13 is clearer, but the problem again is one of context. If we are to embrace Leviticus as 'Holiness Code' for today then we should be very careful about adopting some of it but not all of it. Some of the Levitical codes have a distinct cultural or health emphasis, which may no longer be relevant for today.

It is possible that Jesus makes a passing reference to homosexual orientation in Matthew 19:10–12, where He expounds on different reasons why unmarried people remain celibate (the word used for 'made that way by men' is the Greek '*eunouchos*'). The first two examples ('born that way' and 'made that way by men') given here by Jesus may include people like homosexuals. Certainly the emphasis is on celibacy.

In Romans 1:24–28, sexual orientation is explored in a creation context, where homosexual acts are given as examples of fallen behaviour or unnatural actions. The phrase used is '*para physin*', which means unnatural – opposed to God's nature, rather than to human nature. It is not an issue of what feels natural for you or me. This passage certainly addresses the disobedience of all human beings including those who are practising homosexual activity, and 1 Corinthians 6:9–11 is both specific and pictorial in its language and description of the homosexual act, which it does clearly condemn. It describes an active and passive partner, respectively using the Greek '*arsenokoitai*' and '*malekoi*'. Meanwhile, in 1 Timothy 1:10 the word '*arsenokoitai*' alone is mentioned and this is a direct Greek parallel to the Hebrew word used in the Ten Commandments.

However we seek to contextualise the above passages, three things remain clear.

Firstly, in both Old and New Testament it was homosexual activity which was specified and condemned, it was not people: they were not identified by their sexual orientation. Homosexual as a description of a person rather than an activity is actually a nineteenth-century invention.

Secondly, while only homosexual activity is mentioned and condemned in Scripture, it remains the case that there is *no* underlying distinction made which allows for loving motive as an acceptable basis for homosexual activity.

Thirdly, *all* sex outside marriage is condemned in Scripture; homosexual sex is only one example.

If in reading this you find that you yourself struggle with

homosexual orientation, attraction or temptation, please understand that Christ offers you redemption. But redemption is a process, not a destination. It is a road to wholeness, which only finishes face to face with Jesus, when we either are called to be with Him or He comes again for us. This redemption road is a narrow road and not always an easy option. We follow the narrow road of Christ, not for what He may do in our lives, but for what He has done. And we follow it for theological and not for sociological reasons. So it is important to understand that God says 'no' to homosexual sex, and why. It remains important to continue to share our feelings with God, while at the same time using our minds to listen to His truth. Understanding the needs that homosexuality is seeking to meet in your own life, and understanding how God wants to meet these needs in Himself, are major steps along this road. Learn to listen to yourself and God will eventually show you what He is saying about your self-image, your relationships and your lifestyle. Recognise that if you harbour a low self-image (many with a homosexual orientation do) this will often exhibit itself as a symptom of perfectionism. A perfectionist may demand of God a total change of homosexual orientation, and reject Christianity if this does not happen. Yet the reality is that you are dealing here with the very roots of your sexuality, which may or may not change. The fundamental truth is this: your sexuality is not the root of your identity. Christ is the root of your identity. Your sexuality may be a catalyst for growth whatever its orientation. It should never be a catalyst for rejection and abuse, either of yourself, of others, or of the Church of Jesus Christ towards you.

SOME IMPLICATIONS ...

Let me try and summarise briefly where we have got to so far.

1. Any sexual intercourse outside of marriage is forbidden in Scripture – pre-marital sex means that there is no lifelong commitment (Deut. 22:22–24; Rom. 13:13; 1 Cor. 5:9–13). *Eros* love should therefore be dependent on phileo love reaching a point of lifelong commitment. Whereas premarital sex can end up building a relationship on eros love and not phileo or agape and is unlikely to survive or at least to survive with health. Eros expressed and fulfilled without the foundation of agape and phileo commitment means that you are physically, emotionally, sexually, spiritually and soulishly joined without being committed.

2. The concept of sexual incompatibility is a nonsense! Penises do fit in vaginas and it does feel good! The reality is that the vast majority of sexual problems within a marriage are rooted in the emotional, relational, volitional, rational and spiritual aspects of the relationship, rather than in the physical mechanics or techniques of sex. And the latter are much more easily adjusted than the former.

3. Extra-marital sex is also wrong. Be it sex outside marriage (Deut. 22:22–23; Rom. 13:13; 1 Cor. 5:9–13); same sex sex (Lev. 18:22; Rom. 1:26; 1 Cor. 5:9); sex with animals (Exod. 22:19; Lev. 18:23); sex with violence (Deut. 22:25–27); or sex with family members (Lev. 18:6–7).

4. It is worth noting that eros love without phileo and agape love is wrong even in the context of marriage.

5. The Bible – Old and New Testament – also assumes that the Christian will marry within the household of God.

6. The Bible sees the sexual act not just as penetrative sexual intercourse, but as the whole process of husband and wife arousing one another. So the idea that anything short of penetrative intercourse is OK outside of marriage, is foreign to Scripture. I have had to deal in my own life, and in the lives of many that I serve, with much damage caused by 'heavy petting' committed by 'technical virgins'.

7. Opinions do vary as to how far you relax these principles once engaged, and most certainly – and biblically – they should stop short of penetrative intercourse, but equally certainly it is wise to keep engagements short, so as not to 'stumble', or in rather evocative and biblical terms, it is better to marry than to burn!

'ONE AND ONE IS ALL ALONE AND EVER MORE SHALL BE, OH!'

But where does all this stuff on sex and sexuality fit in if your current status (and perhaps you suspect your lot in life) is singleness? This is a big issue numerically, sociologically and theologically. Thirty-five per cent of adults in the church in the UK are likely to be single, but all too often are still regarded as baby/child-sitting resources and better able to serve because they have more time!

A SNAPSHOT

In information published from the last available census in the UK, more than one in three British adults are single, taking the singles population to over 18 million. It is well known that that figure is now much increased. It compares dramatically with the figure in 1951 produced by the General Household

Survey, which indicated that one in ten adults were single. What is more, it is estimated that by 2020 one in three adults will be living alone. The same government prediction estimates that most women will live on their own and more women will remain childless, according to current trends. This is radically affecting the development of singles' households on so-called Brownbelt areas.

At the date of the last census 48 per cent of men aged between 16 and 44 years were single, compared to 39 per cent of women. With the UK divorce rate now running at 40 per cent, ever more people are becoming single in middle life. The retail industry is a partial measure of this growing trend; Sainsbury's cannot stock enough single prepared meals, and sales of individual half loaves are growing monthly. Nor is the Church in any way exempt from these trends. The survey 'Singularly Significant' indicates that 35 per cent of adults attending evangelical churches are single and the figure rises to 42 per cent in the inner cities. And a Mentel Survey discovered, on a positive note, that whilst 30 per cent of singles cited loneliness as a drawback, 53 per cent said that living alone gave a great sense of achievement and 60 per cent said that they thoroughly enjoyed their freedom.

WHY?

There are complex reasons why these trends seem set to continue. Changing working environments means more responsibility and personal investment for individuals and you have probably found that to be the case in your own life. Greater opportunities exist now than ever before for career and for mobility rather than for family, and pressures on economy produce longer working hours, whilst factors like home-based work, mobility, technology and growing numbers of self-employed all produce greater choice and opportunities for work for more individuals – who often then remain individuals. At the same time attitudes amongst teenagers continue to develop more positively and confidently about relationships; and choosing life with a partner, as opposed to marrying, means that you do not lose your independence. Most of the tax advantages of marriage have been dismantled and so financial independence can be expected and retained alongside growing friendship. Housing policies continue to be affected as women find that they can be financially independent rather than marrying for security.

THE MEDIA MYTH

At the same time and often running counter to God's perspective, our society is very relationship-orientated but pursues experience without context. TV, films, magazines and videos all feature the ideal man or woman, the ideal relationship, the ideal sexual conquest, with enormous peer group pressure on young people to be sexually active. If sexuality is thought to equate to identity then sexual expression is thought to be the antidote to nonentity. So where does all this leave the single, radical, committed follower of Jesus embarking on a life of radical holiness?

DIVERSITY

Well, firstly it is important to recognise that you can be single for a diversity of reasons and with a diversity of experience. You can be single, have never been married and have no sexual experience. You can be single with a history of cohabiting or with other sexual relationships. You can be single, never have been married, yet have a child or children – the 'single/lone parent syndrome'. And you can be single, yet previously married and now separated, divorced or widowed. Some are single by choice, or by calling, which is a voluntary singleness. Others are single by circumstance or for social reasons, which is an involuntary singleness. In all of this, what is God's perspective on singleness?

THE JESUS WAY

By His teaching and His treatment of women (as we have already seen in the previous chapter) Jesus redeemed marriage, and by His singleness He also redeemed that state so both can show God's glory to a fallen world. He followed in a good Old Testament tradition. Jeremiah was told by God not to marry, and in obedience his life became a prophetic statement (Jer. 16:1–15). Ezekiel experienced the singleness of being widowed (Ezek. 24:15–19). When Jesus came on the scene He made God known (contrary to prevailing culture) as a single person. There has never been a person more whole than Jesus and yet He was single; He was not 'half' a person. So Jesus, the world's most famous single person and our best role model, was free to care, free to love and show emotion, relaxed with both single people and married, with men and with women. He related to them with purity and gave them dignity, was emotionally free and demonstrative, welcomed affection and touch and He did all this as a single person. Both Jesus and, subsequently, Paul, spoke on singleness in terms of equal status with marriage. The single person is not half a person, but a whole person. So Paul believed in and promoted both marriage and singleness as valid and equal (1 Cor. 7). On a personal note he goes on to state his preference for singleness and affirms the life of celibacy. These are the goals of the radical disciple who follows Jesus.

UNDER PRESSURE

There is much social and peer group pressure on you if you don't want a 'relationship'. It will insist that there must be something wrong with you (ie you're frigid, or you're gay, or you're mad). Although attitudes are shifting concerning the normality of marriage it is still the case that there is something basically wrong with you from society's viewpoint if you are without a partner at the very least. Certainly you are likely to attract pointed questions from aunts/mums/close friends! Unfortunately, all too often, church is not the exception to these social pressures. Church itself can be very marriage and family-orientated. Meetings can be family-orientated, which is good for a while, but how about meetings without kids? How about breaking some of the stereotypes and roles in church leadership forums? Far too many churches still appoint only men to positions of leadership and too many of those go on to appoint their wives automatically by dint of their relationship! Some have even built up a 'so-called' theology! Some churches deny leadership roles to singles because they are single. Presumably the same churches would have excluded Jesus and the Apostle Paul! The reality is that we could do well to learn from the Old Testament example of David and Jonathan. This beautiful story makes it clear that intimacy does not have to be erotic and the reality is that many single adults are *intimacy* starved rather than *sexually* deprived.

CHURCH AND CHANGE

We need to first change our attitudes, for right attitudes lead to right actions. Single people are not sex mad. Yes, you and I need to be careful, safe and holy in our relationships, but we must not alienate and starve people of love, affection and discipleship, because we are afraid that they would instantly fall in love with us!

We must be actively prepared to develop and release single people into positions of leadership and influence within the church and to provide active role models. At the same time how we do church means that we should be prepared to release single people into demanding careers in the workplace without putting them under unhelpful pressure to attend church meetings. This is of course an issue of both how we regard the workplace – as part of the fullness of God's kingdom – and how we regard singleness.

Care and support for singles should not be expressed simply as mothering or fathering them simply because they have no partner of their own. So friendships, both the same and opposite sex, are very important, as are meaningful touches! Our church teaching programmes need to have more emphasis on singleness as well as on marriage and on inclusive church and to address key issues such as: singleness, sexuality, intimacy, friendship and security. In all of this we should be careful to think through the language we use. Are people truly only a 'family' once they are married? Or does family experientially and biblically have a wider expression? Unthinking phrases can by mistake reinforce the supposed inadequacy of singleness. If church is to change we must be aware of the social pressures upon single people, and if you are single, you will be aware of them already for yourself:

- Loneliness and isolation
- Low self-esteem and value
- Pressure to marry
- Who to bring to a party/event/supper invitation/holiday
- Weddings/Valentine's Day, etc
- Not feeling part of 'family'
- Suspicions aroused about individuals' sexual orientation if they remain single
- Allowing space for single people to form opposite sex relationships without 'match-making' or commenting/gossiping on their every move.
- Awareness that the pressures are different for younger single people than for the more mature. For example, if you are 40, single and longing to be married, then that will require more care and attention, than perhaps an 18-year-old in the same situation.

FOOTLOOSE AND FANCY-FREE!

But ultimately the keys to fulfilment in singleness have to be developed intrinsically and cannot just be appreciated extrinsically. It is more about where you are at on the inside than how people treat you on the outside. So if you are single and truly want to be footloose and fancy-free, here are some final tips:

1. Be positive and not negative. Jesus promised you life to the full, irrespective of your married status, so live it! Being single doesn't mean that you can't relate to married people or to children. Get stuck into all aspects of community and evangelism! Children are not the sole preserve of their parents.
2. The kingdom of God is supremely demonstrated by the

way that we treat one another in our relationships. Friendships are one of the most important parts of your life, but the temptation can be great for singles to develop a low priority for entertaining, for making new friends, and to wait for invitations rather than taking the initiative and inviting people to be with them. A lack of real friendship means a lack of accountability and discussion in your life. It is a weakness that without friendship single people do not have somebody to tell them off or to bounce ideas off or get feedback, or to laugh at them and with them when they are being silly! This is the stuff of life and is not the preserve merely of the marrieds.

3. Don't put your life on hold, waiting until you are married to invest into your life. Do make good friends. Do have a nice home (rented or otherwise depending on what God gives you; this is not inherently linked to whether you are single or married). Do buy good food for other people and have candlelit dinners with your friends and so on ...

4. Do get involved with other families, baby/child-sitting really isn't the only option.

5. Finally, do be satisfied with life. Paul learned the secret of being content with lots and being content with little. Not everything in life is ideal – whether you are married or you are single. We need to come to terms with that. Jesus didn't promise us the ideal. He promises Himself. Don't get stressed and don't get disillusioned – it isn't always great to be single, any more than it is always great to be married. Whatever your status, enjoy God, enjoy one another, enjoy yourself and serve Him.

Chapter 9

SUSTAINABLE SPIRITUALITY?

My friends will tell you that I am not renowned for being the most athletic of individuals! Indeed, if the truth be known, I am of the opinion that most demons from Monday to Friday occupy computers and telephone voicemail systems, on Saturday make a mass migration to the sports fields of the UK, and then on Sundays many are to be found in our churches! However, I do know that some athletes by inclination, build and training, are better fitted to distance running than to sprinting. Very different techniques and very different disciplines are needed by runners, who measure their pace, maintain their rhythm of breathing, measure out their energy levels and are able to move from intermediate goal to intermediate goal, whilst always keeping their focus on the ultimate finishing line. Alternatively, the 100-metre dash requires a brief spurt of intense energy and very high but, in terms of longevity, unsustainable speeds.

My suggestion is that when it comes to the spiritual race we are all running (1 Cor. 9:24–27) we should train and run for the long haul, as though we were completing a marathon. So in terms of our training, our development, our usefulness and our appropriation of resources, we should run the Christian race with longevity in mind and anything different is a bonus (Phil. 1:21)!

BE REAL!

My observation would be that sustainable spirituality equates to personal realities. Any athletes will tell you that they are not only athletes when they are on the track, when they are competing in the race, when they are surrounded by the cheering crowd, when they are spurred on by the comradeship and competitiveness of fellow athletes, but also in the privacy of their own training routine, and when they engage in the discipline of their personal times of rest, relaxation, diet and so on. Now this is equally true for the Christian. Unless our spirituality (by which I mean both the experience and expression of our intimacy with Jesus) is rooted in personal and private realities, then it will be unsustainable. Our corporate spirituality, often evidenced in meetings with other Christians, in prayer meetings and worship times, in teaching sessions given or received, are all vital and indeed are a distinctive of the Christian faith. But our corporate spirituality must be an extension, an overflow, of our personal realities; otherwise the danger is that once the outside stimuli are removed and we find ourselves alone or even isolated, then our spirituality can fade into nothingness.

HOME ALONE

Being alone is not always a bad thing and indeed on occasions is to be deliberately sought after (Mark 1:35; 6:45–46), but being alone can be very different from being lonely. The reality is that, more negatively, at different times in our lives, loneliness and isolation are likely to be our experience. They may be as a result of geography, of timing, of illness, of pressure of prevailing circumstances, or even of persecution. It is at such times that we discover what our hearts' deepest stirrings really are. The Christian on his or her own, at rest, undistracted by external circumstances should always, compass-like, incline towards the same direction, that is to say Godwards.

So in this chapter I would like to propose some spiritual disciplines through which we might find increased freedom. It is true that discipleship and disciples embrace disciplines. But it is also true that disciplines do not need to equate to religious legalism. The purpose of spiritual disciplines is not to make us more spiritual; it is to make us more fully human. Spiritual disciplines do not lead to a healthy spiritual life and a consequential relegation of the rest of life to being fun but not very spiritual! We have seen elsewhere that the concept of spiritual and non-spiritual activities is unhelpful, being more Hellenistic in its ideology than Hebraic. Rather, in Hebrew thinking, God has given us the extravagant gift of life, and to live life to the full means to give glory to God through whatever activity we engage in (Col. 3:17). Since the whole of life is spiritual and every activity has spiritual repercussions, every discipline we engage in has the capacity to enhance our life and celebrate our relationship with God. Depending on our personality and our relationship with Him, some life disciplines will come naturally, whilst others will require a more proactive engagement of our will, leading to 'acts of obedience'. If you and I can become more like Jesus without engaging in some of the spiritual disciplines, then we should be free to do so but experience indicates that discipline is vital. Even Jesus learned obedience through the discipline of suffering (Heb. 5:8; 12:4–13).

So here we go! A whistle-stop tour through some (the list is not exhaustive – only exhausting!) of what I consider to be the key spiritual disciplines.

PARTY HARD

This seems like a good place to start! And you may well find that this is one of the life disciplines that comes most easily. But there will be those reading this book for whom the concept of partying and enjoying themselves is an act of discipline. Either way it isn't optional. Scripture is full of descriptions, illustrations and commands not only to fast but also to feast. The practice of celebration is a vital one. Many of the Jewish highlights in their religious calendar involved celebrations, meals and feasts to remind them of the faithfulness of God and of His provision, and it should be the same for you and me today. As a family we tend to eat 'with thankfulness' rather than 'say grace' at every meal (not least because I don't want my children getting into any kind of religious legalism). But we frequently entertain and always on those occasions begin our meal by joining hands, looking at one another across the table and thanking Jesus for His presence and His provision. There is something special about making all of life an occasion. Any opportunity to celebrate is an opportunity to be taken.

Not all of celebration is about feasting! (Shame, I hear you say!) I would want to include within this spiritual discipline the practice of celebration through praise and worship. On the basis that I don't think you should praise and worship God in public in a way that you wouldn't be prepared to do in private, I would encourage you to celebrate God's intimacy with you through praise and worship on your own in your bedroom. You can dance to God there, sing and shout in English or in tongues, play an instrument, make up a tune, light a candle, listen to a CD worship track, just as readily as you can in a meeting context.

Later on in this book we are going to be looking at the principles and practice of discipling and being discipled. But what about the idea of identifying a 'Joy Mentor'? Of surrounding yourself with people who make you feel good? And what about the deliberate diarying of 'Joy Pursuits'? For some of you this, as much as any amount of prayer and ministry, will be about demonstrating the reality that you have received God's love for you and are embracing biblical self-love. Celebration is a fantastic thing; it is a part of your inheritance, a part of your riches in Christ; it is to be enjoyed whenever possible to enrich your walk with Jesus and give you more to give away, and it doesn't rely upon materialistic selfish hedonism (Phil. 4:12).

Then there is also the celebration of romance! Romance is not about flirtation (which is a sin – treating other people as self-gratifying, ego-boosting sex objects) but rather, in the right context (that of opposite gender, equally spiritually yoked, committed relationship), it is to do with mutual honouring and selfless giving. If you are already in a relationship like this (ie you are 'going out' with someone, engaged or are already married) then I would suggest that romance is part of the spiritual discipline of celebration. Here you are celebrating appropriate intimacy (acknowledging that sexual union is the sole preserve of marriage) and mutual commitment and friendship towards one another. So those are the headlines for the first spiritual discipline.

CHILLING OUT

The second spiritual discipline involves the discipline of rest. The pace of life, like the pace of change, seems to experientially increase year by year. We live in frantic and frenetic times. Yet the practice of peace is not the mere cessation of outward activity. If the practice of peace and rest is not found internally then it cannot be imposed by mere external manipulation. So chilling out is about attitude more than it is about action or lack of it. Connecting to the Great Shepherd of our lives is the best antidote for people who feel helpless and harassed (Matt. 9:36). Some keys along the way include the discipline of 'slowing'. This is the deliberate and conscious discipline and effort involved in learning to live an unhurried life. On average I do between 40 and 60 hours of actual work per week – this is considerably less than I used to do, which is partly as a result of the toll of time(!), but also partly because I have deliberately resolved to embrace the discipline of 'slowing'. I no longer cram my diary with meeting after meeting and activity after activity, back to back and minute by minute. Instead I will allow breathing spaces, unfilled times interspersed between my activities. Having children has helped me enormously in this as there are different times of their day during their development when they need you to be around for them. I do not believe that God has called me to sacrifice my children or my marriage on the 'altar of ministry'. Similarly, having a wife and friends around me who nag at me to achieve this has also helped. In the course of a year I travel 30,000 miles by car around the UK (this is excluding overseas work), and there was a time when I would tear from meeting to meeting up and down the country, always with one eye on the clock (not a good way to drive) and subsequently panic stricken when, not infrequently, stuck in traffic jams. It was with a sense of anxious pride that I could recount how many minutes I had shaved off my latest journey by driving hard! Not any longer; I never set out to be disrespectful to other people's timing, but nowadays if circumstances prevail which are outside my control (that does not include dashing around from thing to thing, which is within my control and which I have stopped doing) then basically 'I get there when I get there'. The reality is that most of the things I go to can't start without me anyway, so there is little point panicking about them!

I have also learnt to be kinder to myself concerning taking holidays with the family. I work hard and I party hard. Nowadays the first things to go into my diary at the start of every new year are holidays and days off. They are not fixed and immutable, they get adjusted, but at least they are in there to be adjusted. I found there to be sobering truth in two statements: 'The graveyards are full of people who thought they were indispensable', and 'You'll always have enough time to do what Jesus has asked you to do'. Although in a different culture, the reality is that Jesus lived His life surrounded by enormous pressures, yet you don't find Him dashing from one thing and one person to the next as you read through the Gospels.

Another aspect of the discipline of peace and rest is solitude. I do feel close to God in a special kind of way when worshipping with 6,000 people in the Royal Albert Hall in London. But it is not the same kind of intimacy that I feel when I take the time and discipline to be alone with God. In fact (and I know this depends partly on personality), I rarely feel as close to God as when I am out alone with Him in the context of His creation. Distractions disappear. 'Hand-me-down' experiences of God fade away and everything gets stripped back to basics – just me and my relationship with my heavenly Daddy. Often linked to this for me is the practice of silence. In a volume-filled, noise-polluted world, silence is an increasingly rare and precious commodity. As a family we have holidayed frequently, and now live, in Scotland (working gradually as we are towards fulfilling the call of God on our lives to that nation) and one of the things I most value about this is the absolute silence that you can find in the Highlands. It is almost tangible; you can drink it in in great draughts. It is like a medicine to your soul.

Isn't it interesting in the story of Elijah, when he is worn out from expending faith, from ministry, from conflict with the enemy, tired, hungry and convinced of his isolation in following the purposes of God, that God chose to minister to him in very specific ways? These included food and rest and the rebuilding of his faith through the hearing of God's Word (Rom. 10:17). But particularly noteworthy is the context in which God spoke. God's voice was not to be found in the whirlwind, it was not to be found in the earthquake. Instead God's voice was the 'still small voice' which came whispering to Elijah's soul in the quiet. The silence of God speaks volumes.

In that same story we find a final aspect of the practice of the discipline of peace and rest. That is sleep! Sleep is God's natural restorative. It is not a kind of 'mini-death' as scientists would sometimes have us believe. It is more to do with life than with death; with restoration and creativity than with destruction. The very first sleep, which embodied all of these principles, was, after all, induced (Gen. 2:21). And so the discipline of sleep provides healing for our minds and our bodies. The personal tension which arises here for me is the balance of celebration and the practice of rest. Given the opportunity I would like my celebration and feasting to go on into the 'wee small hours', but there is a discipline of keeping reasonable hours, of getting frequent good nights' sleep. I can quickly tell the difference when I am not doing that. I can end up snappy and irritable with others; overtired and lacking in energy and spiritual edge during the day; more prone to temptation; more open to inappropriate late-night viewing when staying up beyond the dictates of wisdom. Good sleep and rest is part of God's good gifts to His children (Psa. 4:8; 127:2) and can even be the time when God chooses to further impress His revelation upon us through dreams.

APPROPRIATE SMALLNESS

The practice of servanthood is an essential part of radical discipleship. This is unpacked in more detail in Chapter 11 so a few points will be sufficient here. If we would be great in the kingdom of God, then we must be the greatest servants (Matt. 20:26). This means that we need to embrace the discipline of the mundane. Being faithful in the little means investing in the ordinary. Not all of our life and walk with Jesus will consist of pole-vaulting from one spiritual high to the next! Any race has its highlights and its slogs. So there is a real and freeing discipline involved in investing in the day-to-day 'stuff' of life, recognising that this has enormous potential for shaping our character and making us more intimate with Jesus.

Secondly, there is the discipline of learning to be interrupted with good grace. This often involves the laying down of our own agenda and the serving and embracing of someone else's. It is particularly important if you are of the personality disposition which revels in lists, in details, in projects and in completed tasks. Always remember: people before projects. King David on his way to Jerusalem to be crowned king over the Jews could not find the time to be interrupted by a group of blind beggars. Contrastingly, Jesus

Christ the King of the Jews, on His way to the cross for the salvation of humankind, still found time to be interrupted by one blind beggar called Bartimaeus (Mark 10:46–52). It is also worth noting that we have an inbuilt disposition to believe that our agenda equates to God's agenda! It is a salutary thing, in the context of the discipline of 'chilling out' to sometimes ask God to let you take a peek at His agenda and priorities for your life. My experience indicates that at the very best I usually have to reorder my priorities, and sometimes I find that I am working off a completely different agenda all together! You might try it yourself sometime.

Then there is the practice of 'bearing'. The Bible encourages us to bear one another's burdens (Gal 6:2) and a good spiritual discipline is the shouldering of corporate responsibility, not just the carrying of our own. Since Jesus was reported saying it is better 'to give than to receive' (Acts 20:35) then certainly an aspect of freedom lies in our willingness to give freely of ourselves, our time and our energies to serve and to carry other people's visions and responsibilities.

HOT AND HUMBLE

You might think from all that you have read in this book so far, that the practice of secrecy is anathema to the radical disciple of Jesus. But there are times when it is entirely appropriate to keep certain things 'hidden in our hearts'; indeed Jesus' mother Mary did exactly this herself (Luke 2:19). Following the merging of Church and State with the conversion of the Roman Emperor Constantine to Christianity and the Roman Empire to the Holy Roman Empire, where once it had been life-threatening to proclaim Christianity it now became advantageous. Where once to be a radical disciple of Jesus meant you could lose your family, your job, your possessions and even your life, now it might guarantee you promotion! And so with the synthesis of Hellenic ideology with Christianity, nominalism swept into the Church. Partly in reaction to this, some individuals separated themselves out into a more 'spiritual' mode of existence, with many of them living completely alone in the desert wilderness. There then arose what became known as the 'Desert Fathers', hermits, who for safety's sake grouped together into communities but with minimal personal contact, in their pursuit of union with God. And so the first monasteries were born. It was these same Desert Fathers who explained the connection between secrecy and a heart on fire for God. 'If you want to keep the fire hot, you must not open the door of the furnace too often.' What does this secrecy entail? It means that you embrace the discipline of 'holding your tongue'. For example, if the results of one of your acts of kindness or servanthood are noticed, it means not automatically 'laying claim' to it. It means being prepared to go unnoticed. Alternatively, if you or I are falsely accused, misunderstood or misrepresented, it means not automatically 'shouting the odds' or seeking to justify or defend. Christian writer, Dallas Willard, has it right when he says 'As we practice this discipline, we learn to love to be unknown and even accept misunderstanding without loss of our peace, joy or purpose.'[1]

And the practice of secrecy is also important when it comes to our prayer life. Jesus was very clear; we do not pray to impress others. We cannot pray from a self-righteous attitude. Our corporate and public prayer life should be the extension of our personal prayer life and not its replacement. When it comes to praying we, like Paul, should be 'permanently online' (see Eph. 6:18; Col. 1:9; 1 Thess. 5:17; 2 Thess. 1:11). Given that prayer is emotion as well as words, is listening as well as speaking, we should be in an attitude of prayer at all times. We should be praying with thankfulness. We should be praying with petition (ie asking for things!). We should be praying in English and in the Spirit and in tongues. We should be praying with 'groans too deep for words' (Rom. 8:26) when words will not do.

Jesus made a further connection between the practice of secrecy and our giving. Again the emphasis is not on public giving. Nor is it on the amount of giving; but rather it is on the heart attitude of giving. Our giving must be with generosity and with hilarity (2 Cor. 9:7). The literal translation of this is that God loves a generous/hilarious giver. So laugh till it hurts and give till it hurts! If you are starting out in all this and you want a guideline, then the Old Testament principle was one of tithes (10% pre-tax) and offerings (good will gifts on top of that). Please bear in mind that the New Testament way is better than the Old and you might do well to consider graduated giving, where the proportion that you give increases with the amount that you receive, but 10% is a good place to start! I have never forgotten being asked a salutary question as a student at university, 'If you died tomorrow, would somebody know by going through your credit card slips and cheque book stubs that you were a Christian?' The discipline of generosity with our time, our money, our energy, our friendships, our home, our food, and so on, is a wonderfully freeing one to embrace. I have found consistently that you cannot out-give God, and that in His economy, the issue is not whether I can afford to give generously but whether I can afford not to! The Christian writer, J. Ortberg, sums up this discipline nicely when he writes, 'The practice of secrecy exists to liberate those who are trapped by a desire "to be seen" to impress others. The practice of secrecy is Jesus' gift to approval addicts.'[2]

GIVE IT UP FOR ...

This is a great discipline to practise. Do you, like me, ever get the nagging question as to who is in charge of your life? And I don't mean the hassles and pressures of external circumstances. I mean more in terms of your own internal desires, drives and passions both positive and negative. The Bible teaches clearly that we should be in charge of our bodies and not our bodies in charge of us (1 Cor. 6:12). One of the best ways of breaking the control and consequences of bodily appetites is through abstinence. In other words, starve them out! If that sounds too negative, it is not meant to. The reality is that if you keep a treat as a treat, you enjoy it more. Have it too often, whatever it is, and the danger is that you will come to take it for granted and become blasé about it. A wonderful meal is best enjoyed with the pleasures of anticipation and the building up of appetite. So abstinence is not just about the lack of something in our lives, but more about ordering our priorities, self-control and pleasurable anticipation!

Three key aspects of abstinence then. Firstly, there is fasting. Given that there is no such thing as a spiritual shortcut to maturity, this is one of the nearest things I know to it! Certainly it is clear from Scripture that Jesus intends His disciples to fast – when He speaks of it His comment is 'When you fast' rather than 'If you fast' (Matt. 6:16). In the Old and New Testaments fasting is usually linked to prayer activity. This is in part because fasting in many of its forms creates more time and space for reflection and prayer. It also serves as a useful reminder to us to pray. If you are fasting from food you could match a prayer to every time your stomach rumbles! Of course there is very much more involved than simply food fasting. The fast might be to abstain from all food, or from particular types of food, or from sexual activity for those who are married (supposing that those who are not married are not indulging in sexual activity anyway!). But it is also fun to be creative with the idea of fasting! You could consider fasting from chocolate, alcohol, television. I had a friend who fasted crossing his legs because he had someone in his church who was awaiting an operation and was physically incapable of crossing his legs. Every time my friend went to cross his legs he was reminded to stop and pray for his church member. Medically, fasting is very good for you, providing it is never taken to excess and you would be unwise to fast water intake. If for any reason food fasting is not for you (because of a physical condition, because of medication or because of an eating disorder) then go ahead and fast something else. But fast you should, because it is fun, and because in some indefinable way, by denying one aspect of appetite we seem to sharpen the others. It is like being deprived of a sense; if you are blindfolded in a darkened room it is amazing how much your hearing improves, or your sense of touch. Similarly, if you fast one aspect of your lifestyle it is amazing how your spiritual appetites for prayer, Scripture and fellowship can be heightened.

A second aspect of fasting is the discipline of chastity. Shortly after I was filled with God's Holy Spirit and He began an in-depth work on my character, during my second year at university, I made a vow before Him not to have a girlfriend for a year, which I subsequently extended by a further 12 months. This was in part because I knew this to be an area of weakness for me and a potential artificial bolster to my insecurities, and in part because I wanted to concentrate on focusing on intimacy and time spent with God. That is one form of abstinence. But the discipline of chastity goes beyond this to maintain moral uprightness and purity in our relationships with people to whom we are attracted sexually. Sexual activity (including 'heavy petting' and mutual masturbation) is reserved, for the Christian, to the context of lifelong, monogamous fidelity within marriage. This is because in knowing and desiring the best for us, God has created us to be sexual beings, where our sexuality is an expression of our spirituality. It is in part a symbol of Christ's union with His Church (1 Cor. 6:12–20; Rev. 19:7) but is also the ultimate expression of the nature of God revealed through His creation. Go back and look at Chapter 8. God created both male and female in His image and in our combining together emotionally, relationally, spiritually and physically there is a profound experience, which goes way beyond the physical, and reflects the image of God and created order as it was intended pre-Fall. Any spiritual union outside of God's context is still a spiritual experience, but is no longer reflective of the kingdom of God but rather of the kingdom of the enemy. So chastity is for our best interests. It is the exercising of self-discipline. But more than this it is the honouring in committed friendships of the value of the other gender, providing a safe context for the exploration of friendship and women and men working together and has the potential for healing the battle between the sexes first launched at the Fall (Gen. 3:14–16). Because our culture confuses a person's identity with their sexuality (whereas Christians recognise that their identity is found primarily in Christ and not in their sexuality, expressed or not), and because of the strong biological urges built into each of us by God (the first sexual Being), for many this is not a discipline easy to embrace. That is why there needs to be plenty of room for openness, discussion, honesty, vulnerability, grace, forgiveness, established parameters, explained expectations and, where appropriate, prayer and ministry to cover past sins, hurts and failings.

The third aspect of abstinence is prudence. Prudence is the practice of staying within the boundaries of what is necessary for the kind of life to which God has called us. Practising frugality is not about meanness. It is about good stewardship. It can provide us with the means, even when we have limited resources, of being able to be generous to others. It helps keep in check the rampant spirit of the age personified in consumerism, materialism and hedonism. It is to do with finding enormous pleasure in things that don't cost anything. It is a realisation that you don't have to spend money to enjoy yourself. Or to prove to someone else that you love them; or to prove to yourself that you love yourself. It is to do with learning to be content with little as well as with much. It is not only to do with good budgeting, it is to do with proactively limiting expenditure in order to be able to increase giving. It is to do with capping our lifestyle at a level that saves us from selfish extravagance and the trap of being 'owned' by our own possessions. Let's not mistake radicality for preferential culture. It is easier to be prudent and frugal when you have little or next to nothing, than when you have more. As a student, tithing 10% of very little is very little! Lending a clapped-out old car to someone may cost little in terms of your attitude. It may be that if God gives you favour with your job, blesses you with your bank balance, provides you with a reliable vehicle and so on, the test to your attitude in terms of frugality and generosity will come *then*. Decisions submitted to the Lordship of Christ under one set of life's circumstances always have to be reviewed when those circumstances change, for better or for worse. That's why being a Christian is about being on a journey rather than an arrival.

READ ANY GOOD BOOKS LATELY?

The final, and a vital, discipline I want to encourage you to embrace is the practice of engagement with Scripture. It is unfortunately true that we live in a non-book-reading age. The fact that you are reading this book means that you are representative of a minority. Only 17% of UK adolescents and adults read because they want to rather than because they have to, eg for school/work. Yet in Christianity we are at least in part dealing with a book-based culture. So are there any keys that will help us get to grips with Scripture?

STUDY

It is hard to obey the Word of God if you don't know what the Word of God says. It is hard to claim the promises of God if you don't know what they are. It is foolish to seek God for intuitive revelation about such things as guidance, relationships, morality, finances, when you could simply read what He has already told us! So getting to grips with studying Scripture is essential. This helps us to understand the big picture of God's intervention in human history. It is important that we recognise that the Bible is not a scientific manual; or a technical treatise; or a set of moral propositions. It is, rather, a chronological narrative and you would do well to read it as such. On the DNA course we use resources to help the trainees with this and these include two books in CWR's *Cover to Cover* series, *God's Story* and *Through the Bible as it Happened.*

You might also want to consider one or two other useful

tools in helping you study the Bible. I certainly recommend that you equip yourself with a concordance, which lists the whereabouts of every word used in the Bible and is very helpful for reference and cross-checking, and also with a standard commentary (a good starting place would be IVP's *New Bible Commentary* and their *New Bible Dictionary*). But never substitute the reading of textbooks for the reading of Scripture! In studying it you can of course study a theme, one of the 66 books that make up the Bible, or a character. They are all important, and ringing the changes could help you maintain your concentration; variety is the spice of life!

INSPIRATION

Reading Scripture should not be for study alone, feeding our heads, but also for feeding our hearts. Remember that it is for lack of *vision* or revelation that the people of God perish (Prov. 29:18) as well as for lack of *knowledge* (Hos. 4:6). So we need both. It is therefore entirely appropriate to read God's Word asking His Spirit to fill it and bring it alive to us. This is what I would term more 'devotional' reading and is something that is easy to get into on a regular cycle if you find that helpful. As long as you remember that reading the Bible daily won't make God love you any more. Failing to read the Bible regularly won't help you to get to know the author either! Often in reading the Bible for inspiration we turn to our favourite passages. That alone, however, will likely tend to concentrate your reading in the book of Psalms and in the New Testament letters. So it is *one* way but not the only way.

MEDITATION

This is a great way to cultivate purity of heart and mind. If study is understanding the big picture, and inspiration and devotional reading is understanding the applied picture, then meditation is more about the microcosm. It is a bit like the difference between a sumptuous blow-out at a favourite restaurant (study), a fast-food working lunch (devotional) and a savoured and lengthy enjoyment of one particular dish (meditation)! So meditation would take one particular verse or even part of it and ruminate on that. It would ask the Holy Spirit to speak about the particular words, to nurture, encourage and dwell on the images, picture, emotions and responses that they conjured up. It is not the equivalent of Eastern meditation. That is a process of self-emptying in order to discover the god within you and is inherently dangerous. Rather, Christian meditation seeks to fill the heart and mind with the things and Person of God. In Scripture we are encouraged and exhorted to meditate on three permissible things: on God Himself, on God revealed through His creation, and on God revealed in His Word. So Eastern practitioners might look at their fingerprint pattern and, as their minds go numb and their eyes defocus, they would open themselves up to all kinds of potentially harmful spiritual influences (demonic). But as Christians gaze on their fingerprint whorls, their heart and mind would dwell on the uniqueness of creation and individuality. How they are made in the image of God, how much God loves them as individual and unique persons and so on.

MEMORISING

Finally, an aspect of the discipline of engagement with Scripture involves memorising Scripture. If there is a particular area in your life that you repeatedly struggle with (eg, self-image, sexual temptation, lack of generosity) then a great antidote is to use Scripture as it describes itself, as a medicine (Prov. 3:2, 7–8). Practically, this means to find (here's where a concordance comes in handy!) any references pertaining to that area and then to commit them to memory. It might mean writing them out and carrying them around with you for a while. Eventually, by constant repetition, you will come to know them in your head and your heart, and be able to claim them for yourself; to be able to speak them out in faith against the work of the enemy; to remind God of them as well.

If you combine these four different elements of a disciplined approach to Scripture, it has the potential for liberating you into a passion for God's Word. Just don't let it grow legalistic. Avoid at all costs the condemnation of the enemy, who will seek to tell you that if you haven't had your 'quiet time' today then somehow you are a failure as a Christian. I don't know any Christians who engage with Scripture at the depth and frequency that they would like. Remember that the purpose of Scripture is to be Christocentric. In other words we study it, we are inspired by it and we devote ourselves to it, we meditate on it and we memorise it, because it reveals that supremely it is all for Christ – to us, in us and then through us.

Notes
1. Dallas Willard, I believe this quote is from his book, *Spirit of the Disciplines* (Hodder & Stoughton, 1996).
2. J. Otberg, *The Life You've Always Wanted* (Zondervan, 2002).

Chapter 10

20/20

I can remember when a trip to the optician for an eye test was free. In fact I can remember the early days of working for churches in the East End of London when I was so hard up that occasionally on a day off when none of my friends were around I would pop along to the opticians and get my eyes tested! Sometimes that was my treat for the afternoon! Sad, eh?

Of course those days are no more. Eye tests cost money now. On my last visit to the optician I had my children with me and all three of us had our eyes tested. I am afraid I had left it five years since the previous test and of course my prescription had altered. For years I have worn glasses for driving or the theatre. But I had noticed recently that I couldn't read the channel blurb on our TV screen. So a visit to the optician was called for! But the worst was yet to come. With my new lenses I find that I can see perfectly well for the theatre, to watch TV or to drive, but I can no longer use my glasses for that and then read something close up. My optician broke the news to me gently, that on my next visit it was quite possible that I would need varifocals! I can remember when my Dad first got what were then bifocals –

one of the ultimate signs of approaching middle-age!

But both my children have perfect eyesight, or what the opticians refer to as '20/20 vision'; 20/20 vision means that you have no trouble focusing on the things which are close up, nor on the things which are a long way away. This chapter is about our vision and our focus.

A SHORT STORY ...

'Hallo!' said Piglet, 'what are you doing?'

'Hunting,' said Pooh.

'Hunting what?'

'Tracking something,' said Winnie-the-Pooh mysteriously.

'Tracking what?' asked Piglet coming closer.

'That's just what I ask myself – What?'

'What do you think you will answer?'

'I shall just have to wait until I catch up with it,' said Winnie-the-Pooh.

A.A. Milne, *Winnie-the-Pooh*

Have you ever felt like Winnie-the-Pooh? Something seems missing from life, there is a need for an overall purpose, a sense of direction. You have that sense that if only you could find it, everything would fall into place and life would make sense, but you are not sure what 'it' actually is. You think, you hope, that when you find it you will recognise it. It is a bit like the elusive bit at the edge of a dream; always there, almost within your grasp, but always just out of sight and reach.

Your destiny can seem a bit like that. If only we had clearer vision. Destiny and vision are words bandied around frequently on the Christian scene and indeed in management as well! But what do they really mean. How do we get them?

You have come this far in this book and hopefully you have grown in self-knowledge and self-image, and you are growing in an experience of God as your Daddy and the freedom that brings to our minds, our histories and our choices. You are exploring what it really means to be the woman or man of God that He has called you to be; your identity is increasingly to be found in Jesus. You are finding what works for you when it comes to a sustainable rhythm of life in the Spirit. But here's the question: what is it all *for*?

WHY VISION?

Vision is a view or picture of a preferred future. It is not about what was. It is not about what is. It is about what *might* be. It was Robert Kennedy who said, 'Some men see things as they are and say why. I dream things that never were and say why not.' For the Christian, vision comes from God, but this doesn't mean that it appears in full DVD vision on the plasma screen of the sky! Vision given from God, like guidance, often fits the way that God has 'hard-wired' us. So if like me you love words, then God will often speak to you in words, if you are artistic and creative then God will often speak to you in pictures. If you are of a philosophical bent then God will often speak to you in abstract concepts. If you are very practically orientated then God will often speak to you with concrete expression. And so it goes. However God speaks to you the point is this: vision gives us a focus for faith and faith is an investment that needs continual deposits. Or put another way, faith is a muscle that needs to be exercised. The last time I was in Scotland I had the good fortune to spot an osprey. I eagerly seized a pair of binoculars but found that the bird appeared at first blurred and indistinct and I had to adjust the binoculars to bring it into focus. Vision from God can be like that too. What at first seems to be blurred, indistinct and rather vague and indeterminate, can be brought into sharper focus by a series of small adjustments. Investing faith into vision is what brings it into focus.

STOP, LISTEN, LOOK

What does this mean on a practical level? If you feel that God is saying something or showing something to you, then the focus of faith will firstly mean that you stop and pay attention. Just as when Moses saw the burning bush in the desert he stopped and gave it his time and focus. Burning bushes were not that uncommon in a dry and arid land, so God caught Moses' attention with something with which he was familiar. This was how he was 'hard-wired'. So, starting from a place of familiarity within the reach of Moses' own comfort zone, God got his attention. But what held Moses' attention was the fact that this burning bush did not burn up, and so God moves from the natural to the supernatural. It is the same with the focus of faith. If we will stop from the busyness (or laziness?) of everyday life and give some time and attention to what we think God might be showing us or saying to us, then clarity and definition may be the result.

WAIT AND MOVE FORWARD

But the focus of faith will also require perseverance. We don't always see things clearly straightaway. Sometimes we have to wait. Sometimes, as with my Scottish osprey, the object of our attention is blending too much with the background. Sometimes you can lose what God is saying because of too many irrelevant details or distractions. Patience and perseverance can bring the important into focus from the background of the trivial. But sometimes 20/20 vision will only tell you that you are too far away from the object of your attention and that the only solution for seeing in greater detail is to move forward! Moses didn't only *see* the burning bush, he went up to it. This is an important attribute of vision. As well as giving us a focus for faith, it spurs us into action. We move towards that which we see. We move meaningfully, we don't meander! Vision keeps us on a straight line. Have a look at how this is illustrated in Luke 9:62.

LIKE A TRIG. POINT

Vision also serves as a kind of reference point. If God has caught your attention and you set off towards what you have seen, then the decisions that life throws up become easier to make. Presumably you will make decisions which take you towards the the preferred picture rather than away from it! I used to have one of these car compasses that sticks to your dashboard. When I lived in Portsmouth, I often holidayed in Scotland. You don't have to be a geographical genius to know that Scotland is north of Portsmouth! So for the majority of my journey I would expect to be following a compass pointing North. There would be occasions when the road would twist and turn in some other direction and I seemed to be going the wrong way, but always and overall the direction would swing towards the North and if I was lost and had a choice to make, I would be more likely to take the northern direction than the southern! This is how vision works. There may be necessary detours, but overall our decisions will incline us in the direction which God has shown us. Have a look at Habbukuk 2:2.

You can see therefore why vision is so important. There is no point to Chapters 1 to 8 of this book if we don't know where we are going with it all! And the Bible is clear on this – in Proverbs 29:18 it says that without vision, or revelation, the people of God cast off restraint. The phrase literally means to lose a sense of direction, the equivalent of 'coming off track'. It means that we have no sense of boundaries or guidelines, no parameters to work within or sense of destiny to reach for. Without vision we become purposeless, powerless and passive.

WHAT HAVE *YOU* SEEN?

Has anything caught your attention so far? Have you heard a whisper from God that might become a shout? Have you seen a blur on the horizon that might become a destination? Is there something you are aware of or naturally inclined towards that God might move from the realm of the natural to the supernatural? What would you like your future to look like? It might help you to think about different areas and jot down aspects of your personal vision and it might be helpful to do so along some kind of a time-line. The table below is very practical but could stimulate your thought, prayer and discussion with those close to you.

	1 YEAR	5 YEARS	10 YEARS
Health			
Education			
Skills			

	1 YEAR	5 YEARS	10 YEARS
Job			
Ministry			
Relationships			
Finances			

It would be a mistake to super-spiritualise our understanding of vision. Once we think we have heard or seen something, it really is better to focus on it in faith and start to move towards it, than to do nothing at all. Even if we are wrong, God will find it easier to redirect a moving object than a static one! Don't think that an exercise like the one above is too 'cold blooded'; and how about giving some thought towards some of the things that we can use to help us define our vision and help us to move towards it? Let me give you an example. I had a vision to live and minister in Scotland. I wanted this to involve church planting. I want it to have something to do with business. I would like it to involve community transformation. And it must be involved in discipleship, training and multiplication. Now what would help me clarify and move towards this vision? Well, I needed to be praying into it. I needed to be educating myself concerning Scotland (buying books on the history, researching the culture), I needed to be up there putting my feet on the territory and praying there as well as praying about it. But I also needed to be setting out business plans, investigating mortgages, meeting with bank managers and Christian businessmen. I needed to be making other Christians aware of my heart's desire and vision, so that they also could pray and advise accordingly. Now these are some of the things I could use to help me define my vision and move towards it. I can't do this for you; but can I suggest that you pause and reflect right now? What might your vision be, what ideas/skills/resources can you use to help you define it, and what can you do to help you move towards it?

Please be really practical with this. You might want to take one area from the table opposite, limit it to Year One on the time-line, and then list below three things that you can do to help you achieve it:

1.

2.

3.

ME OR WE?

We live in a very instant, consumerist, materialistic 'me' orientated society. You are not immune from that merely by virtue of being a Christian. We have to choose to be countercultural. The gospel of Jesus Christ is an upside-down approach:

If you want to keep it you must give it away.

If you want to save your life you must lose it.

If you want to lead you must serve.
Instead of individualism we have community.

Have a look at Matthew 6:3 and 16:24–25.

There is a bigger picture here that we need to get caught up in (Rev. 21:1–4). We have a part to play in the unfolding of God's plan. Vision isn't essentially about us achieving our own niche. It is about us finding our role in the drama which God is unfolding against the backdrop of His creation. Our role isn't fixed, it is dynamic. We don't have to fear missing it. God is the playwright who keeps changing the script! But vision is not about Me and Mine, it is about Us. There is a place for personal vision. Without personal vision you will be easily led by others. But as well as personal vision there is also a need for corporate vision. This is not an either/or but a both/and. Personal vision serves to fulfil corporate vision and corporate vision does the same for the individual. Once again it is that wonderful demonstration of interdependence which is a hallmark of Christian maturity. Corporate vision is to do with the direction we embark upon with other people; those that God has called us to and called to us. This is partly the definition of church.

Church is a group of God's people called out with a common purpose/vision (the New Testament Greek word for church '*ekklesia*', from the Greek word '*ek*' and '*kaleo*' meaning to call out from). So when it comes to the specific group of people that God has called you to be with, the particular church of which you are a part, you must be able to understand and 'buy' into the corporate vision of that church. Take a moment to think what you understand that to be; take a moment to answer this question: How can you serve that corporate vision with your own personal vision?

221

Although management gurus have now over-used the concept of vision statements, I do think it is helpful when churches can say succinctly where they are going and what their vision is. For example, the vision of my previous church is 'Love God, Love One Another, Love the Lost'. For many years my own personal vision statement has been 'the maximum amount of God to the maximum number of people'. Does your church have a vision statement? Do you? How do those two combine? You may well find that in your life so far, too much emphasis has gone on your personal vision and that now you need to question how that fits and serves the corporate vision of the people of God to which you are called to be a part. Or you may find that you bought into the corporate vision and you have never stopped to think what your own vision is. To think about that is not to be selfish. If you don't know what your personal vision is you will find it hard to play your full part in the bigger picture. Remember, your personal vision serves the corporate. And corporate vision, because biblical church leadership is about serving and not dominating, should also see you fulfilled, empowered and released to fulfil your personal vision. We need both.

OWNING THE VISION

A few final tips then. When it comes to vision believe in God and believe in God in you. Take yourself and the vision that God has given you seriously. Be neither cynical nor dismissive; He does have a destiny for your life, not a detailed blueprint, but an overall sense of direction and purpose, with good days, good deeds and good gifts for you to move in on. It is very hard for God to lay hold of and use a disillusioned

Christian, so don't be negative when it comes to His vision for your life.

Feed your vision, make space for it, do any homework necessary to encourage it. Read the Bible and pray, align the vision with Scripture and allow it to be shaped by God. And at the same time allow it to be shaped by those around you, particularly those to whom you have given authority. Be humble, don't strive and don't fight the wrong battles.

Avoid faffing around! Don't let passivity, apathy or fear freeze you into immobility. You can be too lazy to inherit your vision or you can be too fearful of making a mistake and missing it – or sometimes even of getting it right! Any of these will produce an inability to act or make decisions. They will promote procrastination and time wasting.

As you work towards your vision be prepared for testing and perseverance. If it doesn't cost you anything it is probably not worth anything. Patience and right timing are needed in the pursuit of vision. Be prepared to allow your vision to be questioned and challenged. Indeed it may even seem to die. But be prepared also for resurrection.

Finally, don't allow Christianity, church and your relationships with others in the body of Christ, become depersonalised. Remember that even when it comes to vision we walk by faith and not by sight. We need to keep in step with the Spirit because we walk by the Spirit (2 Cor. 5:7; Gal. 5:25). In all this it is vital to keep this closing thought absolutely central: *Be close to Jesus. He is the One we follow, not just our vision. Don't live for vision, live for Jesus.*

Chapter 11

DISCIPLESHIP – THE DEFINITION

The danger of talking about topics of discipleship and mentoring is that you and I could be accused of bandying around the latest 'in' phrases. Have you noticed how at the moment everyone is talking about discipleship? And it is not just restricted to the Church of Jesus Christ. In the world of big business, relational management and personal mentoring are cool phrases.

But this book is about being radical. About getting back to roots. My plea is that we realise that there is nothing 'cool' about talking about discipleship. Anybody can talk about it. At the moment everybody *is* talking about it. But in my experience few are delivering it or living with the benefits of it. It is not a current trend. It is not the latest fashion. It is not a peculiarity of a particular kind of churchmanship. It is totally, utterly and thoroughly biblical – and absolutely vital for Christian maturity and fruitfulness. In fact the emphasis in the New Testament is so much on discipleship that it stands out like a sore thumb if only we will take the blinkers off and look. The word Christian, describing the followers of Jesus Christ, is used only three times in the New Testament;

but the word disciple is used 269 times: 67 times in Matthew; 44 times in Mark; 34 times in Luke; 73 times in John, with the rest being in the book of Acts. In other words, in the five key books of the New Testament, which deal with pro-activity, rather than subsequent corrective reactivity (which is what most of the epistles are about), it would be fair to say that a key description of a Christian and the major emphasis of outlived Christianity is centred around the words disciple, discipleship and discipling.

MEANING ...?

Much used though they currently are, the words themselves are open to misinterpretation. Some followers of Jesus would reserve the concept of discipleship for those who would want to be heavy duty, hard-core Christians! And so discipleship is relegated to the realm of those who would aspire to 'full-time Christian ministry' or to 'a year out for God'! Some followers of Jesus would be prepared to embrace this discipleship, providing it were for a fixed and limited period of time and usually associated with conversion, immaturity and baby Christians. Other Christians would view discipleship as a necessary duty; a rather unrealistic demand for an unattainably high standard set by an unreasonable Jesus and His Church! So for them discipleship becomes an unfortunately necessary 'bitter pill' to be treated a little like a course of antibiotics – you have to stick the course to gain the benefits. There are any number of damaged Christians around carrying the hurts and scars of abusive 'heavy shepherding' where discipleship bred dependency, decisions were subjugated to the will of the discipler – for these, discipleship is now to be avoided at all costs.

In reality, and in Scripture, discipleship is none of these things. Its overarching goal is what Paul describes in Colossians 1:28, where he says that he struggles/strives (the impression is of one of hard work) to present every person mature/perfect in Christ. The word used for mature is *teleos*, which literally means perfect, whole, complete. So discipleship isn't an end in itself, it is a means to an end. The end is maturity and wholeness, not dependency. This is found in Christ, so the goal is that we are disciples of Jesus, not of anybody else. The basic aim is to encourage belief in God, a sense of calling and destiny as unique individuals, deepening intimacy with Jesus and ultimately faith in action! John is at particular pains to point this out in his Gospel and letters in the New Testament. This is perhaps why he uses the word more than any other New Testament writer. He has grasped the principle that disciples do not simply believe – they also do.

IT'S ALL GREEK TO ME!

The New Testament Greek word used most often for disciple and discipleship is the word *mathetes*. Like many Greek words this packs several meanings into the one word. Whilst your Bible and mine most often translate the word as disciple, a better rendering would be 'learner/doer'. Immediately the word gives us the clues: a disciple hasn't completed the course; a disciple is teachable; a disciple is likely to make mistakes; a disciple must embrace humility. But a disciple will do all of this in the context not just of introverted, introspective theoretical concepts. A disciple of Jesus will also be an activist, a follower along the way. As the root of the word indicates, disciples will embrace disciplines. They do not learn divorced from reality in some ivory tower. They are not embracing theoretical theological concepts. Their theology must be harnessed to experience. On the other hand, true disciples of Jesus will not merely be activists. They will not simply rush around 'doing' things all the time. They do not merely copy without understanding. They are learners and they are doers at one and the same time.

The other word most commonly used in the New Testament in the context of discipleship is the word *didasko*, which gives us the English word didactic – to teach. Again, a fuller translation gives us a better understanding. *Didasko* literally means 'to extend the hand to someone repeatedly for their acceptance'. This gives us another clue to the meaning of biblical discipleship. Discipleship in essence is relational and not merely informational. It is about personal involvement. It is about perseverance. It is about persuasion and choice, not manipulation and domination. It is about the building of friendships.

IT'S BIBLICAL!

Examples of discipleship in practice litter the pages of the Old and the New Testament. It doesn't take too much reflection to come up with a list of examples. In the Old Testament we see Moses discipling Joshua, Elijah discipling Elisha, Elisha and his involvement with the school of prophets (50 or more). In the New Testament we see that John the Baptist had his disciples; Barnabas discipled Paul; Paul discipled Timothy, and in turn instructed him to disciple others (2 Tim. 2:2). Of course, supremely, discipleship was the model chosen by Jesus as well as commanded by Him (Matt. 28:19). So discipleship is biblical.

NOT AN OPTION

If it is biblical it is *not* optional. Discipleship is an essential requirement of the kingdom of God. It is a part of the great commission (Matt. 28:16–20), which has never been revoked and is still unfulfilled. If it is not optional, neither is it accidental. Disciples are made, they are not born. They are not even 'born again!' Discipleship is not something that happens automatically. Disciple is not another word for Christian. You can be a Christian and not actively engaged in the process of discipleship. Nor do we ever graduate. The style, the method and the people involved in my personal discipleship have altered over the years, but I never should stop being teachable, will never reach the point where I know it all, can never stop serving.

THREE STAGES – THREE KEYS

The journey towards maturity often goes through three recognisable stages. The first is the stage of dependence, when the child is utterly dependent on the parents for the provision of safety, security, comfort, material needs and so on.

The second stage is independence, often marked through the transition of adolescence where the child becomes a youth and pushes the established parameters to determine his or her own personality, individuality, and seeks to establish his or her independence. Many people cease to grow in their maturity at this stage, as indeed do many Christians, believing that ultimate maturity is about their personal and individualised walk with the Lord. Scripture makes it very plain that this is a folly.

The third stage towards maturity is inter-dependence. This embraces personal and moral responsibility, initiative, actions, reactions, consequences and fruitfulness, but does so in the context of relationship with God and with other people. It might be worth a moment's reflection to determine where you fall in this process of maturity.

I'd also like to give you what I (and I think the Bible!) pose as three essential keys in our personal discipleship.

FIRST KEY: DISCIPLESHIP THROUGH SERVING

Have a quick look at Philippians 2:1–18. If ever there was a person who walked this earth who deserves to be served and who is worthy of receiving the deepest outpourings of our devotion, then that person is Jesus. He is our hero! He is our role model. Yet the Bible here is very clear that He came to serve and that as our role model if He came to serve then we should serve. In fact it is explicit in Philippians 2:5, where Paul insists that our attitude should be the same as Jesus Christ's. The word used for 'attitude' is the Greek word *phroneo*, which is another one of those suitcase words, with several meanings packed into the one word! Although translated 'attitude' it would be better to think of the word meaning 'think-feel-do'. So you and I are to have the same 'think-feel-do' as Jesus. We are to think the same way He does, we're to feel the same way and we are to do the same things that He does. This is to be our attitude. So if Jesus is a servant so are we.

There are few better short cuts to maturity than through serving. Jesus, who alone amongst people could have boasted, instead chose to wash His disciples' feet, something only the lowest servant would have to do. If you aspire to discipleship, then you aspire to serve. If you aspire to any form of leadership, influence and fruitfulness, then you aspire to serve. If you aspire to any kind of ministry, servanthood must be your way of life. The very word ministry (*diaconos*) means simply your area of work, of service. So here is a cracking revelation for you: servants serve and leaders serve! In fact, the only valid biblical motivation that anyone can have for leadership is that leaders lead because it is the best possible way at that particular time that they can serve other people. Jesus said it as clear as a bell in Mark 10:42–45 (have a look)!

In my experience, the best way to tell if you have a servant's heart is to wait until someone treats you as a servant and then see how you react. This is because our reactions tell us more about ourselves than our actions. Our actions are the things that in the cool quiet rationale of a godly moment we may choose to do. But our reactions are what spill out of us in the rough and tumble of everyday life and by and large are unpremeditated. And that's why they tell us much about what goes on in our heart. After all, servanthood is not what you would often choose to do, but rather what you are asked to do. Servant-heartedness is about the attitude with which we get on, without conditions and without complaint, which is the attitude of Christ. Going the extra mile beyond that actually means taking initiative in serving, rather than waiting to be asked. It means positively looking to out-serve one another. This then is the attitude of Christ.

HOW TO SPOT A SERVANT

If I litter this book with biblical references it is not to try and prove that what I am saying is scriptural. It is so that you and I might take them to heart and mind, chew them over, meditate on and memorise them so that they might become medicine to our bones and a light to our feet. I can't spell out the characteristics of a servant so that you can use them as a do-it-yourself checklist any better than Jesus did. They are scattered throughout the Gospels, so why don't you look up these references, take them to heart and put them into action?

According to Luke 17:7–10, characteristically servants put their own interests second and their masters' interests first. Facing the discipline of servanthood means going to the back of the queue rather than rushing to the front of it. It means in honour preferring other people above ourselves. It means enjoying it and keeping quiet when other people get the credit even if it is misplaced. And it means being humble and teachable, in putting our hands up if we are at fault when things go wrong. This is because we have a bigger picture of life than merely our own interests. It is because we want to care for and see others succeed before ourselves.

According to Mark 10:42, servants don't fight for status or recognition. This is because true servants have come to understand that their security lies in being part of the master's household and that their safety and identity is to be found in him and not in their function. For the disciple of Jesus, when your identity is rooted in Him it really doesn't matter what you are asked to do, however menial or ignoble, whether or not it is recognised or carries any kudos! Consequently, 'my ideas, my ministry and my opinion', whilst possibly being valid are not the be-all-and-end-all. They are certainly not ultimate truth. They cannot and should not demand and command recognition and unswerving loyalty. Security is found in servanthood and not in status. That is why Jesus, in John 13, could humbly wash His disciples' feet and then in the next breath without a trace of arrogance or selfishness selflessly declare supreme self-awareness, 'You call me "Teacher" and "Lord", and rightly so, for that is what I am' (v.13).

According to Ephesians 6:5–8 you can spot true servants

because one of their characteristics is that they work very hard. But they don't do this as people-pleasers. They don't do it to gain an earthly reward. They don't do it with half an eye out for their own benefit. They work hard as though working directly for Jesus, because they surely are. This is why there is no hierarchy in the kingdom of God. This is why 'full-time Christian ministry' is of no greater worth than 'full-time counter staff at MacDonalds'. Because whatever we do we do it as called by God, we do it for Jesus and to Jesus.

Then in Philippians 2:6–8, it is clear that servants are unafraid or unashamed to get their hands dirty. This in practical terms means that you and I don't just get the nice jobs or the glamour jobs or the jobs that will attract notice. I was recently involved in an evangelistic youth camp where I was responsible for some of our DNA trainees who in turn were leaders of small groups of young people, many of whom did not yet know Jesus. When the drains blocked in the boys' toilets and the sewage started to back-log (and I use the word advisedly!) in the toilet pan, it was the overall team leader in charge of the camp who, with his arms encased in plastic bags, got down to the dirty job of clearing up the mess. Why? He had any number of DNA trainees that he could have asked to do this, they in turn could have asked the kids on the camp. But this team leader had seen something of the 'think-feel-do' of Jesus and decided to adopt the same attitude; the characteristics of a servant with a servant heart – willing to get his hands dirty!

According to Luke 16:13, another hallmark of servants is that they know who their master is. If there is any confusion in your heart or any double-mindedness in your head concerning the ultimate Lordship of Christ (and a better expression would be Boss-ship) you will find that you will use the doubt as a backdoor to bolt through when it comes to aspects of servanthood. But a real servant knows clearly where he or she is indentured. You cannot wholeheartedly serve two masters and neither can I. You have to choose one or the other. You can't have a foot in both camps – you will end up uncomfortably split down the middle.

Finally, in our do-it-yourself checklist on the characteristics of a servant, according to Colossians 3:22–24, ultimately servants know where their reward comes from. It comes from Jesus. In fact you have a choice; you can have your reward now where it is temporary or you can wait and have your reward where it is eternal. Because servant-disciples know that their reward is eternal, that it is assured, that they are never taken for granted, that their very serving can elicit appreciation and even gratitude from the heart of God Himself, then they are not constantly looking over their shoulder to see 'what's in it for them'. They are not disturbed and perturbed even when their serving appears to be overlooked. For in the economy of God nothing gets overlooked, not even our tears.

So if you and I would be radical disciples of Jesus Christ then we must choose to make daily choices to serve. Jesus Himself said it in Luke 9:23–25: 'If anyone would come after me, he must deny himself and take up his cross daily and follow me.' It was the cross of Jesus Christ that effected our salvation. His cross alone is sufficient. So what is the cross that we are to take up *daily*? This is the cross that is to do with choices. It is the crossroads that appears every time my will crosses the revealed will of God. Then I must choose. Do I choose to serve God; or to serve my interests; or even others' interests? Will I be the 'living' sacrifice that Romans 12:1 talks about, even though on a daily basis I might be tempted to keep getting up off the altar?

SECOND KEY: DISCIPLESHIP THROUGH OBEDIENCE

Philippians 2:5–8 not only encourages us to adopt the same attitude of Jesus concerning servanthood, it also encourages us to adopt the same attitude concerning obedience (2:8). An earlier classic book on discipleship by Juan Carlos Ortis said this: 'Many Christians live like the British constitution. The Queen is on the throne but Parliament makes all the decisions.' For the radical disciple this is not an option. When at the age of 17, I started looking around British universities to decide where to go, although I was already a Christian, Jesus wasn't on the throne of my life. Beyond any doubt it was *me* who made the decision as to which university I would attend. It never even particularly occurred to me to let Jesus in on the decision. And if I had and He had said something that I hadn't liked, I am really not sure at that stage that I would have obeyed Him anyway. You see it was easier for me at that time to say I was a Christian than to say I was a disciple; because I was the one but not the other. Jesus was my Saviour, but I hadn't yet understood that for every time He is called Saviour in the New Testament there are a further nine times where He is called Lord which, being better translated, equates to Boss. Discipleship does not only come through servanthood, but also through obedience.

OBEDIENCE MEANS WHAT?

In the New Testament obedience is often demonstrated through moral uprightness or integrity in the big issues of life and the little. An open-hearted reading of Ephesians 5:1–20 provides both an encouragement and a challenge to my levels of obedience.

Let's have a quick look at it together:

v.1 encourages us to be imitators of God. What does this mean practically? It means that every little piece of information and experience I have ever gleaned or enjoyed concerning the character, nature and revelation of God, I copy. And you do the same. But then you see things that I am copying that have not yet been revealed to you, so what do you do? You copy me in as much as I am copying Him. And I do the same with you. This is why real maturity is to do with inter-dependence and not independence. I have never been able to decide whether, as a fashion statement, those little material bands that you fasten around your wrists with the initials WWJD are cheesy or not, but I love the sentiment behind them: 'What Would Jesus Do?' That is a question always worth asking. What's more, on occasions I have often found myself thinking, 'And I wonder what "so and so" would do?' as well. Fill in the names yourself, but it is the people who have most influenced and discipled me in Jesus that I would seek to imitate.

We are exhorted to go on and live as 'children of the light' and I can't stress this enough if you want to embrace the radical discipline of discipleship through obedience. It is not pretending that you and I are the source of all light. No, only God is the source of all light. It is not pretending that we are ourselves luminaries, without spot or shadow. Rather, it is insisting that we bring any dark areas of our lives, of our history, of our experience, our character, our personality, our memories, our thought lives, our relationships, our bank accounts ... into the light of God. It is an exhortation to ditch the negative. Although we happily eat them, the reality is that mushrooms are nothing more than a kind of low-life fungus. They grow in the dark surrounded by manure! In the same way the fungus that would seek to parasitically cling to our own lives grows quickest, and uncontrollably, in the darkness of secrecy and deceit and in the context of waste and mess. It has, I think, been rightly said that it is the unshared areas of our lives that Jesus Christ is not Lord of, and that the blood of Jesus Christ will only cover what we will first uncover. Please think about these statements – they are powerful.

What does it mean then if we sin? If we sin, we sort it out. One aspect of maturity is that we learn to keep short accounts. Our growth in maturity is proportionally related to the brevity between when you sin and when you confess and repent. Radical Christians recognise that sin is not a problem to God. Sin is a problem to us. God dealt with the problem of sin 2,000 years ago and it now is not a problem unless you and I accommodate it. *Having* a problem is not a problem, it is what you do with it. On the discipleship programme for which I am responsible, we try to breed an environment where sin is allowed! Not where it is accommodated; not where it is encouraged. But where the reality of sin is acknowledged, confessed and repented of in order that we might move on from it. Issues ignored and brushed under the carpet simply produce lumpy carpets and sooner or later somebody is going to fall over and break a leg!

v.10 encourages us to find out what pleases God, so whilst we've ditched the negative we need to embrace the positive, and it is not a matter of observation; it is not just finding out – it is also doing it. A friend of mine much used by God was fond of saying. 'Being a radical follower/disciple of Jesus Christ is simple: just find out what God is doing and join in!'

v.15 comes with a warning to 'be very careful, then, how you live'. When it comes to obedience and the discipline of moral uprightness and integrity I think that it implies a degree of alertness, wisdom and effort. On the basis that whatever we do not do in faith is sin (Rom. 14:23) then there is wisdom in living by the maxim, if in doubt, cut it out! So if you are involved in an activity, a relationship, a thought process, financial expenditure, a habit, a place, a hobby, that you cannot do in faith, then you shouldn't be doing it at all. If you are at all in doubt, it is not worthwhile taking the risk.

v.17 is more of a promise than a warning – that we should understand 'what the Lord's will is'. I don't know about you, but I can never think or read about God's will without calling to mind that fantastic definition in Romans 12:1–2 where it is described as 'good, pleasing and perfect'. Another friend of mine has said that the will of God is exactly what you would have chosen for your own life if you had known all the circumstances. I say this because some Christians begrudgingly embrace the discipline of obedience, whereas the Bible is really clear: obedience leads you into the perfect, pleasing and acceptable will of God. Allowing our minds to be transformed and not conformed becomes our spiritual worship, and even under the old covenant in the Old Testament 'to obey is better than sacrifice' (1 Sam. 15:22). Most of us begin our Christian walk of discipleship obeying because we 'have to'. It is admittedly better to go beyond this phase and to learn to obey because we 'need to', ie we reach a point where we have grappled with the deceitfulness of our own hearts and recognise that to please Jesus and to be more like Him we need to obey. But real maturity embraces a third step, which is not obeying because we have to or because we need to, but rather because we 'want to'. This kind of obedience recognises that the will of God is always for us and not against us, that He really does have our best interests at heart, that He really does know what is best for us, and that obedience is, therefore, a doorway into maturity and not a trapdoor into obscurity.

v.18 is the final clincher of this Ephesians passage, where, as Christians, we are commanded, in the present continuous tense, to 'go on being filled with the Spirit'. This is crucial because moral uprightness and the discipline of obedience is not something which we attain by trying harder and gritting our teeth all the more, becoming duty bound, anally retentive Christians! Rather, the only way that this can work is for us on a daily basis to be constantly refilled with the Spirit – the power and Person of God.

THEM AS WELL?

Because radical discipleship is not only about obedience to God, but also to others there are implications here that we need to look at. For example, it is all very well talking about obeying God concerning our own moral integrity, dealing with our own sins, but what if someone else sins? What if they sin against us? What do we do then? Do we have the right to ignore them? To hold them in the grip of unforgiveness (which will always have a stronger hold on us than on them)? To gossip about them? To share information (purely for prayer of course!)? No. The principles of obedience are clearly seen extended in Matthew 18:15–17; 19:16–17: if someone sins against us then we must take the initiative and go to see them. We don't wait until they see that they are in the wrong. Instead, out of faithfulness and obedience we take the initiative in order to win back the relationship. That is the motivation and our attitude must match it. We need to go with humility, acknowledging that we could be wrong, that our perspective may be mistaken, that our reactions may be ungodly, but we do go determined to shape each other to works of righteousness. We make a commitment that we won't push issues under that carpet, that we won't avoid people, that we won't pretend things never happened. This is because in Scripture obedience doesn't only mean moral uprightness, it also means faithfulness. The Parable of the Talents in Luke 19:11–27 is a classic illustration of this. If we will be faithful with the little that God can trust us with, then He will determinedly trust us with more. What does this kind of faithful obedience mean in practical terms? It means that if we are asked to do something then we do it. Not only do we do it, we do it well. If we are asked to be somewhere then it means that we are there. Not only are we there, we are there on time. If we are consistently unpunctual, unreliable, late for people, things and deadlines, then in essence we are not only being rude, we are being supremely arrogant. In effect we are saying that our time is more important than everyone else's. All these things require of us discipline, organisation and perseverance, which is spoken of in Hebrews 12:1–3. Have a look at it. This really is a race; we really do need to run it with perseverance, we really must shrug off the sins that so easily entangle us. In it all Jesus is our example so we keep our eyes fixed on Him. He is our finishing point – the line that we are seeking to cross; the One who always finishes what He starts in us. If we do this we won't grow weary. We might get tired, but we won't grow weary.

WHAT ABOUT LEADERS?

We have already established that biblically the only kind of leadership is servant leadership. This is often said, but too seldom lived out. I am convinced that God is looking for a new kind of humble, servant-hearted leader. For too long in the

Western world and in our churches we have confused personality styles with leadership abilities. It is not insignificant that
the lists outlining leadership qualities in Scripture, to be found
in 2 Timothy and Titus, relate to character and not personality
or function and skills. All too often Christian leadership has
deteriorated into management of people rather than
developers and facilitators for them. The Church has
incestuously sucked people and their resources into its
maintenance and its perpetuation rather than released and
empowered people to more effectively live the life of Christ
outside of church circles in a world that needs to be reached.

Nonetheless there is a biblical principle at work here.
Wherever and whenever you find godly leadership, then you
will also find the discipline of obedience that not only includes
moral uprightness and faithfulness, but also submission.

In Hebrews 13:7 you and I are encouraged to watch,
remember, think and imitate our leaders in Christ and then,
10 verses later, we are commanded to obey and submit to
their authority. Surely it is a rhetorical question to ask you
whether you would like to exercise authority over demonic
powers, to cast out demons, to heal the sick, to raise the dead,
to preach the gospel with signs following – to live the life and
walk the walk and not just talk the talk? If your answer to that
is yes, yes, yes, yes – then you and I have to embrace together
the principle outlined in Matthew 8:5–13. Here you have a
Roman leader of considerable authority and importance,
exercising that position over a 100 or more men; a centurion.
He is not a Jew, but he is clearly a man of faith and wisdom.
For as he looks at Christ what does he say? He doesn't say
what you would expect him to say, or what you and I might
say, which would run something like this: 'Ah, Jesus, I can see
that You are a man with authority. You have only got to speak

the words …' No. He says the very opposite. In effect what he says is, 'Ah, Jesus, I can see that You are a man *under* authority, *therefore* you have only got to speak the word …' The principle is simple, if in the kingdom of God you would exercise authority (and we never exercise authority over people, only over spiritual principalities and powers) then we must be under authority. We are called to honour and respect those who have authority over us (1 Thess. 5:12), recognising that this authority can never be taken, but must be freely given by us. Recognising also that the word used in the New Testament for obey is more often *hupotassein* than *hupokonein*. The first means to be open to persuasion, to submit readily, the second simply means to obey. We are all called to submit our lives to one another in this fashion, not just to leaders. Obeying with this kind of submission does not mean that we lose the right to disagree. But the bottom line is that in the kingdom of God leaders must be allowed to lead. They must be prepared to serve and lead by example. It means that they can expect our obedience, even where we don't agree and not only obedience, but obedience with a good attitude. This is the attitude of Christ. This is also obviously so open to abuse. I cannot outline for you a method of radical discipleship which is free from risk, which does not necessitate faith and trust.

In finishing looking at this second key to discipleship it is worth answering one last question.

WHEN DO I SAY NO?

You see there is a time when you don't obey. When you have to say no instead of yes. You still do so with a good attitude. There is never a time when you are not open to persuasion.

You must never in blind obedience to leadership agree to say, do or be something which violates your conscience, not least because to do so would be to do something which you are not doing in faith and which by biblical definition is therefore sin, even if it is not sin!

It is not even as simple as saying that we say no to things Scripture forbids. For the reality is that there are many aspects of Scripture which are open to interpretation. Now obviously our consciences are not infallible. They are a product of our environment, our culture, our upbringing, our personalities. Nor are they unalterable; they change with experience, with age, with the rhythm of life, with our deliberate choices. But whilst our consciences are not infallible, they are not to be overridden. They may be educated by the things of God, by the witness of the Holy Spirit and by Christians around us. They can certainly be smeared and blunted by repeated sin, to the point where we find it hard to hear from God through our conscience. But the bottom line is that if we are asked to do something which violates our conscience then in all conscience we must say NO.

THIRD KEY – DISCIPLESHIP THROUGH LEARNING

As the father of two children (my daughter Freddi is 13 years old at the time of writing and my son Joshua is 11) I desperately want my children to be teachable. I want them to develop intrinsically rather than extrinsically. In other words when it comes to Joshua riding a bike, I don't want him just to be able to do it because I am running behind him holding onto the seat maintaining balance for him, which would be extrinsic development (and very costly to my general state of health), but rather I want him to maintain his own inner balance and ride the bike for himself (which is intrinsic development). In other words I want them to develop the skills to learn, to explore, to risk, to discover the right questions and not simply furnish them with all the answers all the time. It is a kind father who cuts up the meat on his children's plates when they are four years old, but there is something very odd if he is still doing it for them when they are 18!

And so, the third key to discipleship, bringing us into the process of maturity, is discipleship through learning. And most of us, especially if we have been on any kind of student academic programme had to remember that we need to learn to learn. It does not come automatically. Learning in God's kingdom is not based on achievement, academic or otherwise (rather it is based on availability more than ability). The most useful in God's kingdom are not necessarily the most gifted, but they are the most available. Available to learn and to do. This means that when it comes to our learning there is no room for comparison. Your 100 per cent is the same as anybody else's 100 per cent and so we actively and aggressively avoid the curse of comparison. For the curse of comparison means we will always find people worse off than ourselves, provoking us to pride and arrogance; or we find people better off than ourselves, provoking us to envy, bitterness and resentment.

You can see that Paul knew this very well. He had been well discipled and was a master discipler of many. In 1 Corinthians 9:24–27 you see him lay out some of his principles. These include running to get a prize because he recognises where his prize lies and that it is hard work to get there. It involves him in strict training, with an implicit recognition of 'no pain no gain'! It is obvious that he is able to maintain a sense of perspective and does not waste time and effort on things that are pointless or aimless. He constantly has his goal and targets set before him. He recognises that the light that lies ahead of him is not a train at the end of the tunnel coming towards him! So to this end he embraces the discipline of hard work, he beats his body in order that he will master it and not the other way round. Discipleship is about training/learning.

THE LONG HAUL

So discipleship through learning demands that we take ourselves seriously. It doesn't mean that we are too serious about ourselves, or we lose the ability to laugh at ourselves – where there is little laughter there is often much fear. We recognise that God does take our potential seriously (1 Tim. 4:11–16), so we don't adopt a back-row mentality. We ban phrases like 'I can't/won't do/try that'. We are prepared to pay the price of failure in order to learn to cope later with the price of success. We are people who recognise as we learn (for disciples are learners and wear L-plates) that mistakes are not sin. And we learn not to live merely from moment to moment, but rather refusing to worry about what tomorrow holds we do set faith targets. So you might want to fill in the table below:

---

1. What would you like to do for God in the next …
   (a) Five years

   (b) Ten years

   (c) Twenty Years

---

2. What would you say are the factors that would help you reach these goals?

3. What would be likely to stop or limit you achieving these goals?

CHARACTERISTICS OF TEACHABILITY

It is said that in the first seven years of our life we acquire 66 per cent of our lifetime knowledge. That is a frightening thought when you look at children's progress through school! Could it also be something in the mind and heart of Christ when, in Luke 18:15–17, counter to the culture of His day, He affirmed the right of children to have personal access to Him and then insisted that unless we learn from them we won't even see the kingdom of heaven. Have a think about it for yourself and I am sure that you can come up with a better list than mine, but just what is it about children that give us characteristics of teachability? I would suggest that it certainly includes:

- Enthusiasm (No coincidence that this comes from two Greek words – *en theos*, which means: full of God!)

- The constant asking of questions (I will forever remember the never-ending 'why?' of Freddi and Josh at any and every opportunity!)
- Keenness of observation (My children can quote whole chunks of their favourite videos verbatim.)
- Willingness to copy (Woe betide me if I lick my knife at the dinner table, because I know the kids will follow suit immediately and then we will all get it in the neck from Nikki!)
- A knowledge of where their safety, security and provision comes from
- And more …

AND FINALLY …

In the next chapter we are going to look at some of the principles involved in Jesus-style discipling, ie what we should look for for ourselves and how we should look to serve others that we disciple. But for now let me finish this definition of discipleship by raising our expectations. We should expect to learn, first and foremost, from God who is the Master Discipler. In many respects becoming a Christian is about procreation, new birth. But in many other respects, following Christ is not about procreation, but about parenting and there is no better parent than God, the Father of all fathers, from whom every family on earth derives its name (Eph. 3:14–15). So we should and can expect to be discipled directly from the hand of God Himself.

But we should also expect to be discipled by others – there is that emphasis on interdependence again. Any relationship that you are in has the potential for doing this. Teams have an even more heightened potential. Because of the multiplicity of relational lines, of communication, the potential for the positive and for tensions goes up and we can learn from both. While we are looking at the input of others into our lives I would urge you to answer these following two questions:

- Firstly, who is the Paul in your life, who is giving you input and discipling you?
- Secondly, who is the Timothy in your life, to whom you are giving input, and discipling?

For to receive input without output will lead to stagnation: you will end up merely as a fatter rather than a fitter sheep! Discipleship from others is in the Bible (Acts 2:42–43) called fellowship which comes from the Greek work *koinonicus*, which is to do with being generous towards one another and gives us the word *koinonia*, translated fellowship. So discipleship through others in effect is God with skin on! There are times in our lives when all of us need that. This is perhaps why the name Christian literally means little Christ for that is what we are to be to one another.

However, we can also expect to be discipled through circumstances. Many of us seek to avoid pressure and difficult circumstances, believing them at best to be a hindrance or an embarrassment and at worst to be a direct attack from the enemy. Of course there are occasions when they can be both, but there are also many occasions when circumstances are actually manufactured by God. Wisdom lies in discerning which are which and in not avoiding the pressure, or the pain, or the hard work, that circumstances can throw our way, as even when they come from the enemy, in the redemptive purposes of God, all things can be worked together for good (Rom. 8:28).

Chapter 12

DISCIPLESHIP – THE PRINCIPLES

The apocryphal story is told of a man wandering thirsty through a desert. Suddenly he sees in the distance what he thinks is a mirage, but which proves to be a reality; an ancient water pump set into a rock, a tin container full of water and some carved instructions on a tablet of wood. The instructions read 'Traveller – if you would have much water, first pour the little you find in this container into the head of the pump set in the rock. Thus you will soften and make supple the leather gasket contained herein and water will be yours for the pumping.'

What should the Traveller do? Should he pour away the water that he has and risk getting none back in return? Should he follow the written instructions? Should he take the risk and give away the little he has in order to get very much more? Should he drink or should he pour? What would you do?

The analogy is an obvious one. Do we follow the written instructions of Jesus recorded in Matthew 28:16–20, to go and make disciples; do we give away what we have of God in order to see Him do more? Are we content with our own personal Holy Spirit sprinkling of water, or do we want to be thoroughly soused/baptised with the Holy Spirit? Do we want our own thirst quenched or are we prepared to see streams of living water (John 8) to satisfy the thirst of many?

It was American revivalist and evangelist D.L. Moody who made a similar observation when he asked, 'Should leaders be doing the work of 10 men or equipping 10 men to do the work?' Perhaps it is significant that one of the greatest and best-known evangelists of our day, Dr Billy Graham, once when being interviewed concerning his life and ministry, was asked the question, 'What would you do if you had it all over to do again?' Dr Graham replied along the lines that had he his life and ministry to do all over again, that next time round, rather than simply running the crusades and taking the evangelistic opportunities himself, he would take groups of men and women of God and train them to do what he has done.

The principles involved in discipleship are vital to grapple with. Our commitment to them will ultimately answer the question 'What are we investing in? What is it that we want to leave behind; gold or rubble?' (1 Cor. 3:12). Against the tyranny of the urgent, you and I need to repeatedly hear the call of Jesus Christ to make disciples; to deal with the important and not merely the urgent. It is our task, privilege, pain and pleasure to develop a commitment to be committed to development. If we don't, if we are not prepared to embrace the price of enlargement, then the effectiveness of our lives will be much diminished and in the process we will deny ourselves understanding and experience of the heart of God, which is always for enlargement, always for inclusivity, always for parenting.

Christian writer, J.H. Jowett, said it well:

The range of our possible sufferings is determined by the largeness and nobility of our aims. It is possible to evade a multitude of sorrows by the cultivation of an insignificant life. Indeed, if it be a man's ambition to avoid the troubles of life the recipe is perfectly simple. Let him shed his ambitions in every direction, let him cut the wings of every soaring purpose, and let him assiduously cultivate a little life, with the fewest correspondences and relations. By this means a whole continent of afflictions will be escaped and remain unknown. Cultivate negations and large tracts of the universe will cease to exist. For instance, cultivate deafness and you are saved from the horrors of discords. Cultivate blindness and you are saved from the assault of the ugly. Stupify a sense and you shut out a world. And therefore it is literally true that if you want to get through the world with the smallest trouble you must reduce yourself to the smallest compass. That is why so many people and so many professedly Christian people get through life so easily and with a minimum acquaintance with tribulation. It is because they have reduced their souls to a minimum that their course through the years is not so much the transit of a man as the passage of an amoeba. They have no finely organised nervous system, for they have deadened and arrested the growth of one nerve after another. They have cut the sensitive wires that bind the individual to the race. They are cosily self-contained and the shuddering sorrow of the world never disturbs their seclusion.[1]

But alongside the potential cost and pain of the principles of discipleship, lies the privilege and pleasure. After seeing people saved I know of no greater joy than seeing people brought into wholeness, maturity and usefulness in and with Christ. That has been my experience of being discipled. It has also been my experience of discipling. And it can be yours too.

THE JESUS METHOD

As you might expect, Jesus the Master Discipler exhibits these principles again and again and they can best be seen by trawling through Matthew's Gospel. I am going to give lots of references here, and I urge you to look them up for yourself and let God speak to you in your head and your heart.

First, let's have a quick overview as we dip into the beginning, middle and end of that Gospel. How does Jesus pour Himself away in order that the thirst of many might be assuaged? In Matthew 4:23–5:2 He faces the multitudes with their needs, calls, emergencies and insistences. The same thing happens again in the middle of Matthew's Gospel in Matthew 9:35–10:1 and then again, as if to underline it thoroughly for us, we have Matthew 28:18–20. In each case how does Jesus deal with the demands of the many? He turns away from the multitudes and He turns towards His disciples. In other words His best way of dealing with the need of humanity is to concentrate on multiplying His endeavours through the few.

This is why most of the parables in the Gospels are about multiplication and not just addition. It is not about you and me adding ourselves to the Body of Christ, thereby swelling the ranks of the saved! It is about us being joined to the Body of Christ in such a way that our effectiveness is multiplied into the lives of those who do not yet know Him, and developing the lives of those who do. This is the principle of synergy, where 2 plus 2 does not equal 4, but rather equals 6! It is the same reason that the ministry gifts given to the Body of Christ, described in Ephesians 4:11–13, are about *multiplication* of effectiveness, and not addition. What can we learn about how Jesus did this?

SELECTION

This first principle is well demonstrated in Matthew 4:18. The point is obvious; the disciples of Jesus are *chosen*. This is not an apologetic for Calvinism, as though everything is pre-determined and you and I have no choice in how we respond to Jesus. Far from it. But it is a reminder of the assurance we have that Jesus knows us and our responses to Him through and through, and that we have been selected to follow Him on a wild adventure. That is why He calls Himself the 'way' (John 14:6) and it is, incidentally, why early Christians were called Followers of the Way for some while before they were called Christians (which was initially at Antioch, Acts 11:26). Please note that this selection procedure is a call to follow a Person, not a call to reach a destination. If Jesus had wandered up to me and said, 'Come and follow Me and I will make you a fisher of men', I think that my first question would have been, 'But where are we going?' The call is not to a destination, it is to a relationship (Mark 1:17).

One of the key factors in selecting people from whom we would like to receive or people to whom we would like to give is to be aware of 'people blindness'. Perhaps because of over-familiarity this is what afflicted Jesse when he paraded his sons in front of the prophet Samuel (1 Sam. 16:6–13). He almost overlooked his youngest and least likely son, David, provoking a timely reminder that God does not look on the outward appearance, but rather at the heart of individuals. The implications of all this are very practical, however: in being discipled and in discipling, we should be aware that it will not always work out, we may indeed on occasions lose people. Even Jesus lost one out the Twelve! It is also worth noting that while Jesus did spend some time with Judas, it didn't stop Him spending more time with Peter, James, John and the other eight. So you and I should be reticent to take people on to disciple whose lives are perpetually running in the opposite direction to Jesus as opposed to following Him! There is a difference between spending time and wasting time!

Are there things we can look out for, then, in those whom we would disciple and be discipled by? Well, the early disciples responded to the call of Jesus. So we need to look for responsiveness. We need to look for servant-heartedness (Mark 10:42–45)? They must be people with a heart for God and a willing submission to authority, as well as proving themselves faithful (2 Tim. 2:2). Perhaps above all else they must demonstrate availability and teachability.

It is also reassuring that this call, whilst being personally delivered, is not always to the most obvious of people. It is very clear that the early disciples were not the ideal team! Jesus' Twelve included: two brothers (James and John) who were so often quarrelling with one another that they earned for themselves the nickname of 'Sons of Thunder' (that is what the Aramaic name '*boanerges*' means); Matthew, who was a tax collector and therefore a social outcast; Thomas, who after one incident of being in the wrong place at the wrong time has been cast for all time and eternity as 'Doubting Thomas'!; the ever-vocal but ever insecure and over-the-top Peter, so fragile in his identity that he earns the nickname 'Reed'; and of course it also includes the only named position on the team – that of Treasurer, which is filled by Judas, who ends up nicking the money!

I came upon a spoof memorandum, as though sent by e-mail to Jesus, Son of Joseph, from the fictitious Jordan Management Consultants, Jerusalem, which summarised neatly as follows:

Dear Sir,

Thank you for submitting the names of the twelve men that you have picked for management in your new organisation. All of them have now taken our battery of tests; we have not only run the results through our computer, but also arranged personal interviews for each of them with our psychologist and vocational aptitude consultant.

It is the staff opinion that most of your nominees are lacking in background, education and vocational aptitude for the type of enterprise you are undertaking. They do not have the team concept. We would recommend that you continue your search for persons with experience in managerial ability and proven capability.

Simon Peter is emotionally unstable and given to fits of temper. Andrew has absolutely no qualities of leadership. The two brothers, James and John, the sons of Zebedee, place personal interest above company loyalty. Thomas demonstrates a questioning attitude that would tend to undermine morale. We feel that it is our duty to tell you that Matthew has been blacklisted by the great of Jerusalem Better Business Bureau. James, the son of Alphaeus and Thaddaeus definitely have radical leanings and they both registered a high score on the manic depressive scale.

One of the candidates, however, shows great potential. He is a man of resourcefulness, meets people well, has a keen business mind and has contacts in high places. He is highly motivated, ambitious and responsible. We recommend Judas Iscariot as your controller and right-hand man. All of the other profiles are self-explanatory.

We wish you every success in your new venture.

Yours sincerely

Jordan Management Consultants

Little wonder that it could be said of these guys in Acts 4:13 that when the religious leaders looked at them all they saw was 'ordinary, uneducated men', the literal Greek which is used is '*ungrammatoie idiotae*', which literally means 'ungrammatical idiots'. Yet it was the first principle of discipleship that made the radical difference in their lives; 'these men had been with Jesus'.

What does this mean for you and me? Perhaps firstly it means that when we are seeking to identify our Paul, the person who is discipling us, that we, like Jesus, should first hear from the Father. We should be approaching people (of same gender to avoid complications!) in whom we, like the early disciples with Jesus, see something attractive and of God which we do not have. But we should be doing that after Spirit-led prayer and fasting. This is also true at the other end of the spectrum. When it comes to looking for those whom we can serve and impart to, when we are looking to select our Timothys, the ones whom we are discipling, it may not necessarily be the most obvious of people. But it should always be those towards whom the Holy Spirit prompts us.

We ought also to bear in mind that relationships for us, as with Jesus, operate on different levels at different times. Sometimes there may be an intensity of input into our lives, or from us to others, and at other times that may slacken off; letting people grow in God and letting people go with God is all a part of discipleship. Certainly we must avoid one-to-one lock-ups. So at different times and in different seasons we will receive different things from different people.

Jesus operated His relationships at different levels. He has some kind of relationship with 5,000 people at a time as He taught and fed them. He appeared in His resurrection body to a group of about 500. He presumably had a closer relationship with the 120 disciples in the upper room and perhaps even closer still with the 70 or 72 that He sent out in pairs, representing as they did, all the then-known nations of the world. Certainly He had a more consistent and persistent relationship with the twelve disciples, but even within that group there were the three (Mark 9:2): Peter, James and John, who received particular explanation and revelation. Within the three, Jesus seems to have had a particularly close relationship with John (John 13:23; 19:26; 20:2; 21:7; 21:20).

However, we must beware of setting too high a standard: those who disciple us are human and therefore will have feet of clay! My children have reached the age where they no longer believe that their father knows everything and can do everything and can mend everything! I can't tell you what a disappointment that has been to my ego! However, simply because they realise that their dad is fallible, doesn't mean that they ditch the principle of fatherhood; we are still a family! And at the other end of the spectrum we should be careful that we do not set too high a standard for those whom we are discipling. As you think back over the process of your own discipleship, a good question to ask the person you are inputting is 'Can they do now what I did then?' Or is it the case that as we have all grown and matured in Christ so too we have moved the goal posts and become increasingly less willing to take risks and increasingly more concerned to 'play it safe' in developing others. It is a peculiarity of the English language that the words faith, trust, relationships and discipleship, are actually all spelled the same way: R-I-S-K!

DEMONSTRATION

If the first principle that Jesus employs in discipleship is selection, then the second is demonstration and this can be clearly seen in Matthew 4:23. It was Christian missionary and church-planter, Albert Schweitzer, who said, 'Example is not the best means of leadership … it is the ONLY means.' So again and again in the lives of Jesus' own disciples and then throughout the New Testament, we see the importance of demonstration – leading by example (Luke 11:1; John 13:15; 1 Cor. 11:1; Phil. 4:9).

What is it that we most need demonstrated? We are to be disciples of Jesus and that is what we need to demonstrate to each other. I need to know, you need to know, what Jesus so clearly demonstrated, that our identity in Him comes before our function for Him. That who we are is more important than what we do. That how we do what we do is more important than what we do and that unlike much of the evangelical Church we are not called to lay down our ministries. We are called to lay down our lives and pick up our ministries! That ministry is best discovered in the realm of service, both at the level of the general and the specific. So if my specific ministry is evangelism and discipleship (which it is) that doesn't mean that I can't also set the chairs out! I constantly need demonstrated to me as I need to demonstrate to others, that God will have given me a cluster of gifts that revolve around the ministry He has given me and around my character and personality. So I will be gifted naturally because I have been created by the Father, I will be gifted supernaturally because I have been filled with the Holy Spirit and I will be ministry-gifted by Jesus to get certain jobs done with and for Him. I also need to keep being reminded by demonstration that my experience, knowledge and understanding of Jesus and His ways are not static, but will evolve. That what started off, when I first set out with Jesus, as helpful boundaries to mark the path, will eventually become unhelpful barriers to my further growth and that in every new set of circumstances I need to find God and faith all over again, rather than being depressingly passive and lazy in assuming that, as I follow Him, what was always will be. I must also recognise that when it comes to the principle of demonstration that those whom I lead will attach importance to what they see to be important in my life. If I am not a worshipper of God in spirit and in truth, then those that I disciple will not be either. If I place no value on prayer or on reading the Scriptures then neither will those whom I disciple. The converse is true; if I would develop as a worshipping disciple of Jesus, then I must align myself to a true worshipper. So the principles of demonstration are fundamental – we learn best by watching, by observation and example.

EXPLANATION

Jesus didn't merely demonstrate. He used His examples for explanation and instruction. This can clearly be seen in Matthew chapters 5, 6 and 7. It is worth being aware of one or two key points. Jesus' instruction is primarily and predominantly into character and not just into skills or understanding. This kind of instruction imparts skills rather than simply giving answers, therefore the development is intrinsic and not merely extrinsic. Jesus' explanations provoke moral responsibility, rather than a need to be needed. Discipleship is not about providing a life-support machine, about changing people's spiritual nappies and wiping their spiritual noses! – so when it comes to being discipled, a good question to ask is, 'Am I being directed or am I being developed?' And of those we disciple, 'Am I using these people or am I cultivating them?'

Jesus' instruction of His disciples meant that He shared His life with them, had them with Him, indicating a wise use of time (Mark 3:14). It also meant that while He encouraged their constant questions, He was at pains to answer their hearts and their motives and not just their questions (Matt. 18:1–4). This is a key skill to learn if you are discipling others and an unnerving experience when you are being discipled by someone who knows how to do it! The instruction of Christ carried with it no fear that He would reject the disciples when they got it wrong, nor was it based on a fear that they might reject Him if He had to confront them faithfully. He was prepared to rebuke them in love (Matt. 19:14).

IMPARTATION

Instruction alone is not enough. If instruction (knowledge) deals largely with our heads (Hos. 4:6), then impartation (revelation) deals largely with our hearts (Prov. 29:18). Too much information alone will simply lead to frustration. But information married to revelation will lead to transformation. It is clear in Matthew chapter 10 that Jesus knew how to impart heart burden as well as head knowledge. As our great High Priest, He exercised the same principle as the Old Testament high priests (in Exodus and Leviticus), who went into the presence of God carrying the people of God with them (metaphorically) represented by stones on the priestly garb. They were carried in on the high priest's head and shoulders. True discipleship Jesus-style must be about a sharing of lives, of emotions, of successes and of failures. Not just of theories.

PARTICIPATION

The next step in Jesus' principles of discipleship is that the disciples participated in the 'stuff' that Jesus is about. You can clearly see the progression as you go through Matthew 10. From being mere observers the disciples are now involved in the action for themselves, albeit in a safe context monitored by Jesus. Any process of discipleship that you and I are receiving or serving others with must involve this element. It may feel risky. It can be scary; it is open to failure. But this is the real arena of training and learning. Everything else up to this point has been in the realm of the theoretical and the possible. Participation brings it into the realm of the immediate and the real. Most disciples are happy to go along with the process up to this stage, but when participation kicks in they/we can often kick back! As a disciple, you must be prepared to bite this bullet. As a discipler you must be prepared to fire it!

REFLECTION

This should follow on closely after participation and is an essential part of any educational process. As disciples, we must avoid the risk of being doers only, as opposed to active learner-doers. Jesus consistently had His disciples report back to Him. They were enthusiastic about the stories of demons cast out and sicknesses healed. But they were also bewildered about some demons that wouldn't shift. This afforded Jesus the opportunity for further instruction and impartation ('This kind only come out with much prayer and fasting' – Mark 9:29). You and I must cultivate the habit of learning to learn, of reflection. This is often best done as close as possible, time-wise, to the lesson experienced in order to capture not only the details, but also the emotions involved. Often it is best done in some kind of written form so that we can look back on it, as can our discipler. Written records build faith. We will come back to this point in the next chapter. If we are to be like Jesus, then reflection must not be an end in itself, but must trigger holistic feedback. By which I mean, comment not only on what happened, but why it happened, how it happened, what the feelings and motivations involved were and what we would change for the better next time round.

DELEGATION

By the time we reach the end of Matthew's Gospel, chapter 28 verses 16–20, we see a supreme example of delegation. This is the step beyond mere monitored participation. It is the actual handing out of the jobs to the people whose characters can best deliver.

But Jesus' principles of delegation carry some important learning curves for us. Perhaps the first, and one of the most costly, is that delegation demands that we give away decision-making power. So if something is delegated to you by your discipler then along with that should go the right to take whatever decisions are required to get the job done according to the values that you and the discipler have both embraced. Values are not the same as methods. So the decisions that you take may be different to those that your discipler would take, and your discipler in delegating stuff to you doesn't give away the right to question your decisions, but at the end of the day it is better that some decisions are taken rather than none at all.

Our second learning curve in the principle of delegation is that trust stimulates security and disarms fear, whereas mistrust breeds stagnation. We can only be discipled and we can only disciple others in an environment of trust, encouragement and affirmation. This is a safe environment which recognises that mistakes are not sin and that the worst thing that can happen is that it all goes horribly wrong! But that doesn't jeopardise relationships. *Kakohaphaeo-phobia*, or the fear of making mistakes, will freeze people into impotence. In this environment failure becomes a positive learning experience and has the potential for being redemptive. So instead of failure becoming a trapdoor to obscurity, it becomes a doorway to maturity. The problem with delegation is that the failure of others can reflect badly on us and our tendency therefore is to play it safe and rein them in! It is easier to drop people than to get them to do things properly. But people must be allowed to fail in the same way that people must be allowed to sin. Otherwise no one will ever risk anything or confess anything. The only thing that we must beware of is of rationalising failure instead of facing up to it and therefore rationalising ourselves out of obedience. Have a look at how Saul made his excuses and ended up in disobedience (1 Sam. 13).

The principle of delegation also teaches us that those on the job are likely to be the ones with the best ideas. This is because when God calls He also equips and to those who have the vision goes the job! This therefore demands credit and recognition where things work, and covering and accountability where they don't. We must also learn to give up good jobs as well as bad ones. Sometimes delegation is a poor excuse for giving away all the crumby mundane jobs that we don't want to do! But a discipler must be prepared to give up good, exciting, rewarding jobs too, and aware that this may well provoke flashes of their own insecurities in the letting go and giving away.

Perhaps a final point to make on the principle of delegation is that although you can delegate jobs you cannot abnegate responsibility. This is why when delegation works, the person you are discipling gets the credit and when it fails you get it in the neck! It is a great way of keeping humble. It is worth bearing in mind, in the way that Jesus employed delegation as a principle of discipleship, that in the short term, it doesn't work. In fact in the short term delegation is a nightmare. Things don't get done, or they don't get done as quickly or as well. But in the medium to long-term, delegation is the only way of producing effective disciples. People can, through effective delegation, gain a sense of their own gifting and usefulness to God and others; they too can serve. It means that 'all the jobs haven't gone'. It means that people can get faith and vision for their own part in God's destiny. It means that things won't always be done your way, they will be done differently, but that doesn't mean that they will always be done worse. In fact on many an occasion they will be done better. Delegation is a breeding ground for humility. It is an antidote to indispensability. Remember the cemeteries are full of people who thought that they were indispensable to the purposes of God!

I hope that that has been a helpful look at the Jesus principles of discipleship. Each time I have described one of these principles I have tried to make it cut both ways. So as you read through this I would like you to apply it in two directions at once. Are these principles being outworked in your own life by the person/people discipling you? Are you employing these principles actively in the people you are discipling? I would like to think that this chapter and the final one will provide you with helpful checklists to see how well you are being discipled and how well you are discipling others.

1. Dr J.H. Jowett, *The School of Calvary* (Schmul Publishing Co., 1988).

Chapter 13

DISCIPLESHIP – THE PRACTICE

I was in a meeting recently with a bunch of the people on DNA (the year out discipleship programme) and had the privilege to witness a very special moment.

We had been looking together at gender issues, singleness, women in leadership and ministry, sexuality and women and men working together. It had been an intensive day and as we neared the end of the evening session the presence of God came heavily on us and it seemed appropriate that some kind of response was made that would better reconcile men to women and women to men. Humility, vulnerability and repentance were needed on both sides as oppressions were identified, hurts were healed, manipulation was broken and tears flowed. In the midst of this one of the trainees brought a prophetic word which she felt God had for those present. As she began to give it, nervously and a little shakily at first, her eyes welled up and she began to weep and weep. Much was going on, but one of the things that I suddenly realised was that the reason why she was so impacted by the word she was delivering was that as she gave it she realised that it was as much for her as for those who were listening to her. It is a fantastic and humbling thing how in the economy of God His dealings through us for others often have the remarkable ability of bouncing back and dealing with things in our lives too.

Now the final chapter of this book is a little bit like a double-edged sword as well. I would like to use this chapter to describe the practice of discipleship as though it were you and I discipling someone else. This is entirely appropriate as it takes the focus off us receiving all the time and puts it healthily onto us giving to others. As long as we remember that that which we are giving out to others and expecting them to receive from us, we should first be receiving from those who have access into our lives to disciple us.

ESTABLISHING PARAMETERS

So what is the first thing that I will do if I am about to embark on the exhilarating journey of discipling another? A couple of years ago someone in a position of responsibility and leadership in our own church approached me and asked if I would be prepared to disciple him on a personal and functional level. It so happened that his area of ministry, like mine, was evangelism, and he was keen to be expanded in usefulness, but aware that there was a connection between usefulness and character development. Now when he initially rang me up to ask this question, I didn't really know him at all. I had probably met him in one or two public meetings since he had moved to the area and prior to that I had had no contact with him at all. My response, therefore, was to express my gratitude (and surprise!) at being asked and, to give the request its due seriousness, that I would think, talk and pray further and then get back to him with a decision. Obviously what I wanted to do was assess how much time I could commit to this and to hear from God concerning the process of selection, as outlined in the previous chapter. I also needed to make sure that other people involved in his life (his cell group leader and congregational leader, for example) were happy with my involvement. Having done all of this, I was then able to get back to Ian and happily agree to serve him in this way.

The next thing we did was to book up an evening together and go out and chat over a curry! It was at this point in the natural flow of conversation that I was able to establish what for me are five critical parameters when it comes to discipleship. Please don't misunderstand me (and please don't simply try to replicate this by rote); I didn't work through these things on a list, but did make sure that we had covered the ground by the time the coffee and hot towels arrived!

The first thing that we talked about was friendship. If indeed, as we have seen earlier, it is true that to teach or disciple someone means to repeatedly extend the hand of friendship for acceptance, then friendship has to be one of the first parameters. It doesn't mean that everyone that we disciple (or are discipled by) will become our 'best bosom buddy' and whilst some friendship can occur naturally, *all* friendship has to be worked at. So our commitment together was to begin to explore and work at friendship. This means, on a practical level, ensuring regular contact. It means sharing time together that is not simply 'issue' based, but which also includes social time. In Ian and my case it would also probably mean our wives getting to know each other, finding areas of interest and overlap (which in our case seems to largely revolve around eating curry and drinking wine!). It would certainly also involve kindness, thoughtfulness, the taking of initiative one to another and not leaving it all to flow in one direction. Certainly it would involve generosity (who is to catch the bill for the first curry?) and it must involve mutuality.

This is a lesson I had previously learned in my early days of discipling, when James, the person I was then seeking to serve brought me up sharp by observing that we seemed to have entered a relational 'one-way street'. In other words I always had much to give him, much to tell him, much that he could learn from me, many ways in which I could serve him. But that one-way flow is not conducive to the building of friendship. Even socially I had taken the lead and initiative. It wasn't until James was able to say to me 'Let me teach you about the kind of music/sport/hobbies that I enjoy so that you can receive from me' that I began to realise my error. I wasn't about to repeat it now with Ian!

The second thing that Ian and I talked about that night was the right to speak into one another's lives. Again it had to be a two-way understanding but the principle had to be worked out in practice. If I saw something in Ian's character, his understanding or his skills set, which I felt was lacking then I had the right to speak into it. If this parameter is not established then the whole exercise becomes futile. It must be established embracing the reality that speaking the truth to one another in love will on occasions be painful. But if it comes out of a context of growing friendship then it is a manifestation of faithfulness, rather than confrontation. Well, by now we had finished our first pint of Cobra, had demolished the pickles tray, crunched our way through the poppadums and the prawn puree was but a memory! As we moved towards the Dansak, I began to talk about another important parameter.

Encouragingly, I suggested to Ian that discipleship was about being given the permission to 'drop people in at the deep end'! To his credit Ian didn't go too pale although that might have been more to do with the lime pickle than the threat of being 'out of his depth'! If the principle is that people only develop once they are beyond their coping mechanisms and familiar security barriers, then the practice is that we need to identify or create situations and be prepared to place people in them to see how they might grow and develop. The next parameter went down a little better as did the Peshwari Naan. If the threat for the disciple is that you will 'drop them in it', then the promise is that if necessary you will 'pick them up'. So Ian and I talked about the context for discipleship being a safe environment. If much was being asked of Ian in terms of his character, understanding or skills growth, then much would have to be provided to ensure that he was safe and secure even if uncomfortable, that his successes would be celebrated together and that his failures would be covered.

That led us neatly into the fifth parameter over coffee, when Ian and I took a quick look at the nature of mistakes. My take on mistakes is that you cannot grow and develop without making them; that discipleship demands experimentations without the promise of success. That indeed we learn as much by our failures as we do by our successes. Because Ian's value in God's and my eyes was not based on his performance equating to his worth, and because rejection was not up for negotiation, fear of failure could be begun to be worked on. Within these parameters mistakes therefore ceased to be a stumbling-block and became a stepping-stone. They are no longer a trapdoor into obscurity, but a doorway into maturity.

And so ended our first meal together, the beginning of building what has proven to be a real and lasting friendship, which has certainly proved valuable to me and has in some ways been of service to Ian. At the end of that first curry I asked Ian to think, talk and pray on what I had said and then come back to me with a decision about whether he wanted to proceed on the basis of those parameters. This he subsequently did.

IDENTIFYING GIFTING

Now, because no one gets discipled in a vacuum, a vital second stage in the practice of discipleship is to identify areas of gifting, as often this will provide the 'handle' on a person's character; it is the context within which he or she will be developed. But if you don't know the person, how are you to identify his or her gifting? There are various questionnaires which you can fill in to identify people's aptitude in areas, for example, of spiritual gifts. However, I confess that I have found them to be rather restrictive and sometimes even prescriptive and I would prefer to suggest three simple methods, which I think are rather more flexible and open to the Holy Spirit of God.

The first is to simply question them. This is clearly a Jesus method (have a look at Mark 5:30; 6:38; 8:5; 8:23; 8:29; 9:21 etc.). There are many occasions when Jesus asked questions of His disciples, His followers and even His protagonists. In doing so He wasn't simply playing games with them as though He already knew the answers because He was fully God. Rather it seems to be that because He was also fully human He asked the questions in order to acquire answers that He didn't know. We don't need a word of knowledge for everything! Think back to the first couple of chapters of this book and the various exercises that I suggested that you embark on. They were to help you to acquire self-knowledge and understanding. You could do exactly the same things with people that you are discipling. You could ask them what they perceive their strengths to be; not only in terms of function, but also in terms of character. What do they think their weaknesses are? Which list is the longer? What is it about God that really makes their heart race? What is it about the outworking of His kingdom that gives them the greatest thrill? Find out about their dreams, their hopes, their ambitions; ask them about their frustrations, their disappointments and their fears. What about their job and their past jobs? How about past experiences – what has been formative in their lives to date?

Secondly, however, you will want to identify gifting not merely by questioning but by revelation. This was the other prevalent Jesus method (have a look at Luke 13:10–13; John 4:16–19). This revelation can be direct from God to you through spiritual gifts such as a word of knowledge, prophecy and the distinguishing of spirits (which are among the revelation gifts listed in 1 Corinthians 12), or it could be through indirect revelation, ie prophecies that the individual has received previously from God through others. Certainly I would always want to know what prophetic words are over the life of the person I am discipling and I would want to know that in specific terms and not just generalities. The questioning can tell you a lot about people's maturity and give you clues for areas of development if in their reply they are not able to point you to a prophecy book or file which they have already been keeping.

The third way in which you can identify the gifting of the person you are discipling is through observation. This is best done in a variety of settings and through good use of time. So with Ian, for example, I have wanted to observe him in the context of praise and worship, at home with his wife and children and parents, as he relates to his lodgers, how he treats people in restaurants(!), how he responds and reacts to me (in my good and my not so good moments!), in his work setting (he is a dentist; in fact he is my dentist!) and, more latterly, in the context of public ministry in teaching and evangelism.

Before we move on it is worth pointing out that we should be looking to identify gifting in individuals' lives in three arenas:

- They will be naturally gifted by God the Father in character, personality and skills.
- Secondly, they should, can and will be exercising spiritual giftings from the Holy Spirit (eg Rom. 12; 1 Cor. 12).
- Thirdly, the Spirit of Jesus (Eph. 4) will have given them areas of work or service (*diakonos*), which will be their ministry gifts. These are often an accumulation of and are built on their natural and spiritual gifts.

Finally, it is worth also remembering that the gifting and calling of God is irrevocable (Rom. 11:29) and therefore that gifts given can remain in operation, but they are not static. They can be added to, built upon and developed and therefore if you have been discipling anyone for any length of time, it is worth reassessing what their gifting has become and not just continue to work with them on the basis of what their gifting once was.

ACCESSING OPPORTUNITIES

Only someone who is perfectly mature can lead another into perfect maturity. It has not escaped the attention of my family and friends that I am not yet that person! And if you are reading this book, then I guess that neither are you! Indeed the only fully perfect human being who has ever lived was Christ Himself. Ultimately it is He we all follow. That is why Jesus has disciples and I don't. I can disciple others and they can follow me in as much as I follow Jesus, but they belong to Him and not to me. They are His disciples and not mine. He is all they need. I am not. What this means in practice is that you and I will be discipling people whom we cannot develop holistically. There will be areas of their gifting, personalities and characters that we are not the best people to address. This is of course one reason why real discipleship should never lock in simply to one-to-one. A responsible discipler, spotting such areas in the life of the one he is seeking to serve should be active and prepared to take initiative in accessing opportunities for those areas to be developed by others. With Ian I could do much of the discipling myself, as his gifting as an evangelist is similar to mine, but I well remember discipling Andy, who was very different in personality and in gifting to me. One of Andy's gifts that needed developing at the time I was serving him was that of worship leading. I am not a worship leader. But I know a man who is! So I arranged an introduction, a meeting, and talked through some parameters and expectations with my friend Bob, a worship leader. Consequently Andy benefited, I saw him grow and enjoy that, and the church was the better off for his enhanced ability to see what the Holy Spirit was doing in the leading of worship. His development was not restricted to discerning the anointing of the Holy Spirit in meetings, however, for Bob was also able to develop him in his technical ability musically. A good discipler thinks through who he knows and what opportunities he can create or open up to those he is discipling and is constantly prepared to 'let go and let grow' just as parents with their children.

REFLECTION

We have looked at the importance of reflection for you and me in previous chapters, and if it is important for our development, then it is going to be important for the development of those we are seeking to serve. For now, let me mention just two important aspects of reflection. The first is to do with the importance of questions. In the early 1980s when I was working for Youth for Christ in the East End of London, the Director of Staff Development was a wonderful man of God called Ken McGreavy. Ken was kind enough to let me latch onto him on a regular basis so that I could learn from him and be discipled by him and indeed Ken has influenced me enormously as a spiritual father. When I first started travelling with him to some of his ministry opportunities I would carry his bags and sit in his car racking my brains for the most appropriate and clever questions to ask him! Imagine then my horror and surprise when I found myself being bombarded with questions from him! I can remember thinking, 'It is not supposed to be this way round – I'm the one supposed to be asking you the questions. After all you're the one who is supposed to have all the answers!' But Ken had understood an important principle; by asking me questions he was reinforcing the concept of reflection, at the same time as pointing me in the direction of the best questions to ask! It was a principle I had to learn over many years of ministry – if you have the right questions you are more likely to get the right answers. Of course, he did encourage me to ask questions of him and as I grew in confidence I certainly took the opportunity to do that. Our discipling of others needs to encourage their detailed questioning of not only what we do, but why we do it and how we do it and what motivates us. At the same time they must be prepared for us to question them.

Jesus did this all the time (Matt. 18:1–4) although you will often find that He answers the heart attitude behind the question rather than the question itself, which is very frustrating when you are reading Scripture and must have been terrifying for the questioner! I have always encouraged people that I am discipling to question me in this way: 'Why did that work? Why did you do that that way? Why did that not work? What were you feeling just then?' and so on. And so my car on the sometimes-long journeys to and from ministry opportunities becomes an integral part of the discipling process just as much as a formal training session would or a frank eye-to-eye 'hot-seat' session. Indeed I once had an occasion when a female I was discipling (alongside a male I hasten to add) infamously explained to a public meeting that she 'learned more from Pete Gilbert in the back of his car than anywhere else'! It is on such comments that ministries founder!

The second key to reflection I would like to mention is that of the importance of recorded work and experience. If the person you are discipling is literate (and that shouldn't be taken for granted) then this can take the form of a 'portfolio' of their discipling process. Included might be a project that you have asked them to describe, illustrate, explain and write up, linked to their gifting or to a ministry opportunity you provided them with. Perhaps something connected to the values and ethics behind their workplace. Or to the way that they handle finances. It might be a book, video or tape review of something you have asked them to study which is particularly germane to their character development. Or perhaps you have asked them to prepare a talk to give in the context of a college Christian Union, or a church cell meeting, or church celebration. Maybe it would be personal reflections or a meditation on a Bible passage or verse that you have asked them to look at, or a character from Scripture. Whatever it is, the value and discipline of constructing a record of reflection is a vital part of growth. At the very least I would always encourage someone I am discipling to maintain a spiritual journal which is kept on a minimum weekly or (preferably) daily basis and is very much more than a retrospective appointments diary! Rather it should reflect on what God is saying to them, doing in them, how they are feeling, their reactions to that which they encounter, what succeeds, what fails, their relationships to others, prophetic words, highs and lows ... In the early days of establishing a relationship with someone you are discipling (if that is not already in place) then their journal can become an excellent opportunity for them to 'shop themselves' as often times people find it easier to allude to problems that they might have in writing rather than come out and say it to you face-to-face.

Of course, if they are not literate, then there are other opportunities and avenues open for them to continue with the process of recorded reflection. On the DNA Year Out Discipleship Course we have trainees whose first language is not English; we also have dyslexics. And it is sometimes easier for them to keep a record of their reflections on tape, be that video or audio.

FEEDBACK

The final thing I want to leave you with concerning the practice of discipleship is the vital importance of feeding back at any and every opportunity to the person you are seeking to serve. There is nothing worse than someone seeking to develop if they feel devoid of any points of reference and any kind of assessment, including positive criticism. If you and I are going to give critical feedback, however, it is vital that it is couched in the framework of approximately three positive statements for every negative one. At a time when I was training and discipling a number of school workers I became renowned for the phrase 'just a few things however ...' This was because in any sit-down feedback session I would major on the positives first finding any and every opportunity I could for praise, encouragement and affirmation, then always finish up with the phrase above, which would be followed by a list of areas for improvement.

The very name of the character Barnabas in Scripture indicates that he had a ministry of encouragement, which I think is a wonderful thing and one we should all seek after. It is certainly a vital tool for the effective discipler. It is a fantastic thing to see the one whom you are discipling grow in confidence, self-respect and ability as they flourish under the positive and warm glow of approval, acceptance and affirmation. I cannot stress this enough.

Feedback should also however include the element of correction and adjustment and should be meted out in the context of friendship, because we are prepared to be faithful to those whom we are discipling. Although there will and should be elements of confrontation in discipling, they will be palatable if the person we are discipling knows that we have their best interests at heart and are seeking to empower and release them rather than direct, control and manipulate them. It is trust which stimulates growth and mistrust which stagnates it.

Just as with reflection, so too it is important with feedback that some elements of it are recorded. I think if I am asking people to undertake the task of writing or recording their thoughts and actions, then I should at least be prepared to do likewise with some of my comments. Practically, this means that I will mark work which they do, I will read their journals and comment on them, I will on occasions give written reports and assessments concerning their skills, understanding and character development – certainly this is something we do on a termly basis in the DNA Discipleship Year.

The last practical tip I would leave you with is this. Always end time spent with the person you are discipling pointing them clearly and directly towards the next step, the next phase, the next season, the next practical action, which they can embark upon in the journey of their discipleship. Never leave an individual standing still, at a loss to know where to go to next, what to pray, what to read, who to see, and so on. Even if it is only the date of the next time that you will meet with them. Or when you next want to read their journal. Or when you would like to hear them give the Bible study you have asked them to prepare. Or what book you would like them to read on what topic. Or when they can come round so that you can cook them a meal. Or when they can do your garden.

In all of this I have found the practice of goal setting to be absolutely vital. If you don't like the concept of goals, call them faith targets! Call them what you will, but for goodness sake do be prepared to set them for the person you are discipling. Please make sure that you are setting SMART goals. SMART goals are as follows:

Specific – the goal you set must not be vague and woolly, nor must it deal with generalities, motivations or emotions only, but it must be detailed.

Measurable – it will therefore have quantifiable criteria within it, which means that you and they will be able to assess whether or not they have attained the goal.

Attainable – SMART goals are attainable goals. Because to

set goals which are unrealistic is to set yourself up for failure, disappointment and disillusionment. To leave room for further development and for God to do the impossible beyond our possible (therefore ensuring that there really is an element of faith involved) I would normally set a goal at about 75 per cent attainable and seek God or push myself the next time for the further 25 per cent!

Relevant – the goals that we set for ourselves and those we disciple must be directly related to the area of development we are seeking and must serve not only the point of departure, but also the desired point of arrival; ie, the goal should not be confused as an end in itself, but rather as a means to an end, that the goal is the method to get us to the vision and should not be mistaken for the vision itself. Always measure your goals against what you want to see delivered ultimately and thereby keep them relevant.

Time-related – SMART goals always have a time-frame built into them by which point we can assess how much of the goal we have been able to achieve and to stop us from the debilitating affects of keeping on working at the same thing without discernible progress. Indeed the whole of the discipleship process should be time related and not continue *ad infinitum*.

So there you have it! Five keys to the practice of discipleship. We finish the book in what I hope is a very practical way, but I didn't want to flip into method without establishing definition and principles first. Otherwise the danger is that we become human 'doings' rather than human 'beings' and then the danger is that in our discipling of others we are reproducing after our own kind!

END WORDS

That's it for now! I want you to know that I didn't write this book just to fill my time and your bookshelves! I wrote it for YOU. I wrote it because over the years God has been incredibly kind and gracious in developing me first-hand, but also second-hand; 'God with skin on'. Over the years He has put around me many people from whom I have been able to learn, glean aspects of the character of Jesus, copy in terms of skills, grow in terms of understanding. It is my greatest prayer that He will do the same with you. I know it to be His desire. The question is, will it be yours? If I could somehow take the truths and tips contained in this book and implant them physically into your heart I would reach off the page and do it. But I can't. So I leave you with a prayer that God will grow you as a daughter or son, that you will find out that the Christian life really does work and that it is a lot of fun. And that whatever happens, our destiny is secure as His kids. Thanks for allowing me the opportunity to share with you some of the mistakes and lessons that I have learned, in the hope that you can avoid the one and embrace the other.

Pete Gilbert can be contacted at PO Box 58, Chichester, W. Sussex PO19 8UD for bookings related to discipleship, evangelism, leadership, training, church strategy and structure.
The DNA year out discipleship programme can be accessed through www.dna-uk.org

National Distributors

UK: (and countries not listed below)
CWR, Waverley Abbey House, Waverley Lane, Farnham, Surrey GU9 8EP.
Tel: (01252) 784700 Outside UK +44 1252 784700

AUSTRALIA: CMC Australasia, PO Box 519, Belmont, Victoria 3216.
Tel: (03) 5241 3288

CANADA: Cook Communications Ministries, PO Box 98, 55 Woodslee Avenue,
Paris, Ontario Tel: 1800 263 2664

GHANA: Challenge Enterprises of Ghana, PO Box 5723, Accra.
Tel: (021) 222437/223249 Fax: (021) 226227

HONG KONG: Cross Communications Ltd, 1/F, 562A Nathan Road, Kowloon.
Tel: 2780 1188 Fax: 2770 6229

INDIA: Crystal Communications, 10-3-18/4/1, East Marredpalli, Secunderabad –
500026, Andhra Pradesh. Tel/Fax: (040) 27737145

KENYA: Keswick Books and Gifts Ltd, PO Box 10242, Nairobi.
Tel: (02) 331692/226047 Fax: (02) 728557

MALAYSIA: Salvation Book Centre (M) Sdn Bhd, 23 Jalan SS 2/64,
47300 Petaling Jaya, Selangor.
Tel: (03) 78766411/78766797 Fax: (03) 78757066/78756360

NEW ZEALAND: CMC Australasia, PO Box 36015, Lower Hutt.
Tel: 0800 449 408 Fax: 0800 449 049

NIGERIA: FBFM, Helen Baugh House, 96 St Finbarr's College Road, Akoka, Lagos.
Tel: (01) 7747429/4700218/825775/827264

PHILIPPINES: OMF Literature Inc, 776 Boni Avenue, Mandaluyong City.
Tel: (02) 531 2183 Fax: (02) 531 1960

SINGAPORE: Armour Publishing Pte Ltd, Block 203A Henderson Road,
11–06 Henderson Industrial Park, Singapore 159546.
Tel: 6 276 9976 Fax: 6 276 7564

SOUTH AFRICA: Struik Christian Books, 80 MacKenzie Street,
PO Box 1144, Cape Town 8000. Tel: (021) 462 4360 Fax: (021) 461 3612

SRI LANKA: Christombu Books, 27 Hospital Street, Colombo 1.
Tel: (01) 433142/328909

TANZANIA: CLC Christian Book Centre, PO Box 1384, Mkwepu Street,
Dar es Salaam. Tel/Fax (022) 2119439

USA: Cook Communications Ministries, PO Box 98, 55 Woodslee Avenue, Paris,
Ontario, Canada. Tel: 1800 263 2664

ZIMBABWE: Word of Life Books, Shop 4, Memorial Building,
35 S Machel Avenue, Harare. Tel: (04) 781305 Fax: (04) 774739

For email addresses, visit the CWR website: www.cwr.org.uk

Day and Residential Courses
Counselling Training
Leadership Development
Biblical Study Courses
Regional Seminars
Ministry to Women
Daily Devotionals
Books and Videos
Conference Centre

Trusted all Over the World

CWR HAS GAINED A WORLDWIDE reputation as a centre of excellence for Bible-based training and resources. From our headquarters at Waverley Abbey House, Farnham, England, we have been serving God's people for 40 years with a vision to help apply God's Word to everyday life and relationships. The daily devotional *Every Day with Jesus* is read by over three-quarters of a million people in more than 150 countries, and our unique courses in biblical studies and pastoral care are respected all over the world. Waverley Abbey House provides a conference centre in a tranquil setting.

For free brochures on our seminars and courses, conference facilities, or a catalogue of CWR resources, please contact us at the following address. CWR, Waverley Abbey House, Waverley Lane, Farnham, Surrey GU9 8EP, UK

Telephone: **+44 (0)1252 784700**
Email: **mail@cwr.org.uk**
Website: **www.cwr.org.uk**

CRUSADE FOR WORLD REVIVAL
Applying God's Word to everyday life and relationships

CWR's Online Bookstore

Christian resources for everyday life and relationships

Offering a complete listing of all CWR's products, our Online Bookstore includes:

Our latest releases

A bargain basement

Forthcoming titles

Personalised pages

CWR'S ONLINE BOOKSTORE

www.cwrstore.org.uk

KISS AND TELL
Pete Gilbert

Pete Gilbert believes that effective evangelism springs from a close relationship with God. This book is perfect for helping individuals and groups explore the subject of evangelism and learn to present the gospel in a way that others will understand.

ISBN: 1-85345-285-8
Price: £7.99 (plus p&p)

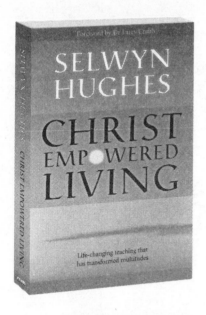

CHRIST EMPOWERED LIVING
Selwyn Hughes

Christ Empowered Living is Selwyn Hughes' dynamic core teaching in one easy-to-digest volume.

It will transform your life with essential principles of Christian living and develop you to your full spiritual potential. You will discover biblical insights that will revolutionise your approach to the way you live and help to renew your mind.

This new edition improves readability and gives larger margins for notes.

ISBN: 1-85345-201-7
Price: £7.99 (plus p&p)